THE OFFICIAL HANDBOOK FOR NEW HOME SALESPEOPLE

BOB SCHULTZ

Bob Schultz & the New Home Specialists

PUBLISHING GROUP
a division of New Home Specialist Inc., Boca Raton, FL

Acknowledgment

While first putting this book together, I was reminded many times of something someone once said to me as we sat in a huge football stadium filled with people; "Isn't it amazing how many people you *don't* know."

Well, I want to acknowledge a few of those people that I *do* know who encouraged, inspired and worked with me on this project. First, Mr. Ken Behring, the guru of volume building for whom I first sold new homes, his Vice President of Marketing, Ken de Board, who in 1969 hired me, a wet-behind the ears kid (and professional jazz musician at that) fresh out of college, and the late Jerry Franklin, my first sales mentor. They gave me my first new home sales opportunity.

It is with much appreciation that I thank Mr. John B. Deinhardt, my friend and mentor. My years with him at Multicon, Inc., were rewarding, both personally and professionally. My understanding of home building and development as a business and my appreciation of negotiating as a game came from him.

To my friends, Rock Lubin, who encouraged me to become a sales educator and real estate consultant, and Tom Hopkins, who first suggested that I write this book, many thanks for all your inspiration.

I owe much to my friend, Nido Qubein, and the late Tom Watson of Creative Services, Inc., who edited and helped with all aspects of this project. Next, much appreciation and gratitude is given to Peggy Burkett Schultz, my friend, wife and Vice President of our company for all of the guidance and encouragement she gives me.

Finally, sincere thanks to the many thousands of new home salespeople, managers, marketing directors, Realtors, builders and all others from around the world who have attended my seminars and programs and with whom I've had the opportunity to work with and learn from.

The Official Handbook For New Home Salespeople is for you!

9th Printing, February 2006
This edition published by New Home Specialist℠ Publishing Group, a division of New Home Specialist Inc.
2300 Glades Road, Suite 400 West
Boca Raton, Florida 33431, U.S.A.
E-mail address: info@newhomespecialist.com
Website: www.newhomespecialist.com

CONTENTS

SECTION IV
CLOSING THE SALE

SECTION V
MASTERING YOUR MOST POWERFUL SELLING TOOL: YOURSELF!

Preface

THE CHALLENGE OF NEW HOME SALES

"There are only three things to know about how to get what you want. ***One,*** *decide what you want.*
Two, *decide what you are willing to give up to get it.*
Three, *go for it."*

H.L. HUNT
Texas Oil and Real Estate Billionaire

Why this book? Why a ninth printing? More than 500,000 new titles come off the world's presses yearly—— 80,000 or more of them in the United States —- why one more? Why ***The Official Handbook for New Home Salespeople***? Permit me to give you five significant reasons.

1. **We can no longer afford to do business as usual.**

   The "roaring" 1990's were a great time to be in new home sales. In most parts of the country, everybody was buying and everybody was selling. As Woody Allen once said, "90% of life is just showing up." Many of us were just plain lucky to be in the right place at the right time, with good models, a good economy and highly motivated buyers. For several years annual housing starts hovered well above the 1,000,000+ mark. There were healthy price appreciations and in some markets sales were easily facilitated. Because of this, some new home salespeople greatly confused the size of their paychecks with their level of skill.

   However, the marketplace in the new millennium is changing dramatically. We can no longer accept "Status Quo". We now find that selling new homes is something that has to be worked at consistently and diligently. We have to work hard and smart to succeed, and constantly be willing to ask ourselves this question, ***"Doing what I'm doing, the way I'm presently doing it, how many sales am I missing."*** More and more builders and Realtors are taking a pro-active attitude toward the selling process. Since its first printing, thousands of salespeople, managers, Realtors and builders have acquired this book. Now in its ninth printing, the strategies and techniques contained in it are as valid as ever.

   I have been involved in new home sales and management for more than three decades. Today I see more enthusiasm among the people entering our industry than at any previous time. Making a lot of money in a very satisfying business is a prime motivator.

2. **As an owner of a marketing company which focuses on sales training, sales management, on-site management and marketing.**

   I see the new home building and real estate business expanding and maturing like never before.

   Each year I speak to thousands of builders, sales managers and new home sales representatives who attend my seminars around the world. Even the best salespeople are increasingly seeking to improve their skills in marketing management, understanding today's buyer, advertising/ promotion and sales management strategies.

3. **The art and science of selling new homes has changed rapidly during the last five years.**

In a supercharged, highly competitive marketplace, salespeople who still use yesterday's techniques are finding themselves being bypassed by fast-track professionals who have learned this foundational principle: You don't succeed as a new home salesperson by manipulating or conning people into purchasing what you want them to buy.

You prosper when you serve, when you assist them in recognizing their housing challenges and as you show them how those needs can be satisfied. You thrive as you learn to maximize your presentation and people skills.

4. **Our industry is plagued by widespread mediocrity.**

Why? It does not take a college degree or any standard of performance to become a new home salesperson.

Anyone who can pass a state's licensing requirements can, in fact, call himself/herself a real estate salesperson.

Let's use Jane Q. or John R. Public as an example. He or she signs up with ABC Real Estate School. During the coming weeks, they spend 80 hours of classroom time studying many technical aspects of this business — abstracts and deeds, land ownership documents and description of lands — but zero hours in the analysis of selling skills.

They graduate and take their state licensing examination, passing with flying colors! "This is great!" they exclaim. "We're *real estate salespeople.*"

Wrong! Their license certifies that they have at least a minimum proficiency in technical knowledge, but hardly proves that they know anything in the area of people skills or selling prowess.

What happens? They get a job selling new homes with the second builder to which they apply. They learn a few pertinent details about the company's five floorplans. Within a week they make their first sale to a young couple who listens to the rambling presentation and write out an initial deposit on the spot!

"This is great"! "We're *professional* real estate salespeople."

The first month, they sell two more homes. By the second quarter, they are edging past some of the company's veterans in terms of total sales. At the half-year mark, they receive a plaque for their achievements.

"This is great!" "We're *successful*, professional real estate salespeople."

Wrong! In all likelihood, they have reached a level of proficiency known as "unconsciously incompetent."

If their story is similar to 95% of the salespeople I counsel, the problem is that they are making sales, yet not understanding why. But because they are making sales, they think they are successful.

In truth, since they are an example of an average salesperson, they are producing one-third to one-fourth the sales that they could be closing if they only understood the fact that selling is a science and an art, and if they mastered the necessary skills.

In my travels I see so many real estate salespeople like Jane and John who get licensed, obtain a job somewhere and reach a moderate level of success. Face it: Anyone who is alive and on the job, regardless of abilities or conditions, will make some sales. People are going to buy houses, no matter how much or how little the salesperson does. Here is the question that needs to be asked: How many people did Jane or John fail to close?

I am alarmed at the mediocrity which abounds in our industry. I continue to see companies who base "success" upon what their representatives sell, rather than the efficiency of the sales force.

Salespeople must learn to equate success in terms of the *conversion ratio*. We must ask how many concluded transactions a person makes in relation to the number of presentations.

The conversion ratio should be the critical test. Since it is not in most sales offices, mediocrity abounds.

That must change!

5. **I have been asked repeatedly to put this project together.**

Companies have asked me to assemble the materials used in my seminars and client consulting sessions to help novice representatives get started properly and to assist top-flight professionals set new goals.

Why ***THE OFFICIAL HANDBOOK FOR NEW HOME SALESPEOPLE?***

Theory is fine, but I have sought to put together the most comprehensive, practical material that will accelerate your career. I purposely stay in the real estate "trenches" as much as my schedule will allow. Believe me, I know what it is like when you face the new, savvy breed of prospective buyers. I know the exhilaration that explodes when the agreement is signed. I know the lowest-form-of-low you feel when hearing "no" for the fourteenth time in a row.

My travels carry me from Florida to California, and from Arizona to New York. I present seminars for the National Association of Home Builders and to salespeople for companies all around the country. I can say without reservation that all new home salespeople confront similar obstacles, regardless of floorplan, price or location differences. You are the reason I have written this book.

What can you expect in these pages?

You will be introduced to a higher level of awareness about your career and challenged to achieve your highest potential as a sales professional.

You will be shown how to always be prepared to perform, psychologically and emotionally, and how to make a qualified and organized presentation to anyone at anytime in a minimum of five minutes!

Special emphasis will be placed on overcoming objections. You will be given effective, proven tools to get your customers involved in the product, to own that new home (even before they buy it!) and to make a positive, mutually-satisfying decision.

Who should read this book?

I have written in general for anyone who earns their living or whose income is directly dependent on the result of a sale of a new home. While many of the strategies explained in these chapters may apply to sales of all real estate, the focus of this book is on selling new residences — single homes, condominiums, planned communities and resorts.

Remember, professional selling is both an art (personality) and a science (process). You can't effectively practice the art until you have mastered the science. You must be willing to commit to a continuous course of learning. As Pat Riley, the legendary coach in the National Basketball Association says, *"There is no such thing as status quo. On any given day, you're either getting better or getting worse."* One of my mentors, dear friend and colleague, Tom Hopkins, has taught for years that we must "PDR" (Practice-Drill-Rehearse). That advice is as important and critical today as the day he first said it.

Specifically, I have targeted this book for the *"slight edge"* person who is not content with average sales. There are lots of "order takers" or "facilitators" in our industry, but ***The Official Handbook for New Home Salespeople*** is aimed notably for the salesperson who desires to be in the top 5%. Only you know whether you are dedicated to making serious money and if you are willing to "PDR" to reach championship status as a new home salesperson.

Are you still willing to accept my challenge? Remember H.L. Hunt's words which introduced this Preface:

"There are only three things to know about how to get what you want. One, decide what you want. Two, decide what you are willing to give up to get it. Three, go for it."

If you have already sorted out that first point — if you want to be a great new home salesperson — then let's get started. Best wishes as you begin your journey through ***The Official Handbook for New Home Salespeople***. May you have a lifetime of successful "Main Event" presentations and enjoy huge earnings.

Bob Schultz, MIRM, CSP
Boca Raton, Florida
March, 2001

THE TWO BIGGEST SALES
YOU WILL EVER MAKE
Selling Yourself on Selling,
Then Selling Yourself to the Customer

Chapter One

A NEW HOME SALESPERSON?

"Persons who reach the top rungs in business, management, selling, engineering, religious work, writing, acting, and in every other pursuit get there by following conscientiously and continuously a plan for self-development and growth."
—DAVID J. SCHWARTZ, Ph.D.[1]

SHTICK!

There is nothing quite like being a new home salesperson.

To your sales manager, you are a pin on the sales analysis chart. To corporate bookkeepers, you are an item called "cost-of-sales." To the customers who walk through your model home, you are either Atilla the Hun or Mother Theresa. Simultaneously, you must be a dazzling orator, necessary nuisance, design specialist, financial analyst, marketing consultant, verbal trash pile and statistical encyclopedia.

To succeed in new home sales, you need Tom Hank's impish charm, Glenn Close's cunning persistence, Muhammad Ali's powerful endurance, Shirley MacLaine's esoteric introspection, Billy Graham's evangelical zeal, Bette Midler's brassy attitude, Tom Cruise's deft delivery, Whitney Houston's warm elegance, Stephen Spielberg's creative genius, Michael Jordan's dazzling moves and Jim Carrey's madcap flair!

You must be impervious to insults and indifference, able to deal with anger and scorn, ready to handle complaints and objections --- and you have to do it with compassion and finesse.

You probably wish that your homes had a few more benefits, the prices a little lower, your commissions higher, your competitors more ethical, your sales manager extra sympathetic, your company's advertising more glitzy and your customers slightly more human.

You must be a realist --- accepting the fact that you live in an imperfect world (though you are expected to be infallible!).

Each morning you hoist onto your back the dead weight of last month's sales record and the burden of next week's quota. Yet, for all that, you have to be an eternal optimist --- hopeful for today and absolutely certain tomorrow will be better.

---

1. David J. Schwartz, Ph.D., The Magic of Thinking Big (Englewood Cliffs, NJ: Prentice-Hall, Inc., 1959), p.56.

CHANGES

As a new home salesperson, you face a rapidly changing marketplace. Your life, in many ways, is affected by factors which are largely out of your control — consumer trends, interest rates, building supply shortages/surpluses, population shifts and job demographics.

Customers, for example, are different today than they were five years ago. They are busier, more selective, often impatient with those who waste their time. They are competitive shoppers, wanting the best price and expecting the highest quality.

The prospective buyer expects more than a slick pitch from you. Television (an average of seven hours a day — that's a daily dose of one and a half hours of commercials) and increased education (86% of all adults now have high school diplomas and nearly 20% have college degrees) have altered the view of selling forever.

And if your sales pitch is geared toward getting Mister Average to buy a house for Momma and the kids, think again! The traditional American family — a dad who works, a mom who stays home and their two children — is fading fast. Although 81% of families are still headed by a married couple who live together, 52% of married women with children under the age of six now work. Furthermore, 16% of families are headed by a woman without a man in the house. And nearly half of the 2.4 million new households are headed by women.[2]

On top of that, the number of couples becoming parents for the first time is rising sharply (of which 15% or more of whom are unmarried). A lot of people who delayed having children are getting around to having their first, helping to create the highest rate of first-time parents since just after World War II. (What do we call *this* trend — the "Baby BOOM-boom?")

These patterns point toward massive changes in the sales of *all* real estate.

---

2. "The Way We Are," Universal Press Syndicate, January 9, 1987, p. 12B.

NEW HOME SALES

In addition to facing the trends and challenges already mentioned, ones that every real estate representative encounters, you have at least six hurdles that existing home salespeople don't face:

1. *You must deal with the difference between the real and the imaginary.*

HURDLE: An existing home comes with an established neighborhood — good or bad — with a proven resale value. A new residence is largely sold as a conceptual projection.

ADVANTAGE: You are offering something brand new! Your customers will help bring a community to life.

CHALLENGE: Sell the dream! Talk about the new amenities. Build excitement about selecting colors, wallcoverings and carpet. Help the customer mentally move into a never-lived-in home.

2. *You must deal with more "just looking" shoppers.*

HURDLE: Who hasn't gone new house browsing "just for the heck of it?" It hardly requires a commitment to jump into the station wagon, drive over to the model home and drop in for a moment. Calling a Realtor and requesting an appointment to see an existing home, however, often signals a definite interest in buying.

ADVANTAGE: Good advertising brings lots of prospects through your doors. Customers feel less pressure, because they know (and they know that you know!) that they can leave any time they want.

CHALLENGE: Your demonstration skills must be superior to resale agents. You don't know whether that person who is "just looking" will buy or not. Therefore your ability to showcase your product must always be ready to "shift into overdrive."

3. *You are generally limited to a fixed location.*

HURDLE: While the resale specialist is free to romance the customer, you are married to your merchandise. Unless your company is offering two or more communities at one time, you have little flexibility.

ADVANTAGE: Unless your builder has an unlimited number of floorplans, you have a distinct opportunity to know more about the homes you are offering than the resale agent who may not have even visited the existing home before showing it.

CHALLENGE: You must know infinitely more about your models merely to be competitive with the agent who has thousands of MLS listings available.

4. *You usually have firm price structures.*

HURDLE: Since your prices are fixed, negotiations cannot center on the amount your prospect will pay for the home.
ADVANTAGE: Your resale counterpart must learn to wrangle with an array of terms, prices, offers and counter-offers.
CHALLENGE: You must develop an attitude of offering a multitude of other valuable benefits. (Notice, not features, but benefits.)

5. *Your customer governs the selling situation.*

HURDLE: Unlike the resale agent who sets appointments, selects showings and drives the prospects to homes, your customers arrive in their own cars, inspect the property at their convenience and leave when they want.
ADVANTAGE: Your personal transportation costs are reduced, plus you can limit time with recreational "lookers."
CHALLENGE: You must qualify quickly, involve more participation, make a condensed, dynamic presentation and close superbly.

6. *You must defend your company as part of your demonstration.*

HURDLE: Resale professionals can side with the tastes of the customer, since they have a large number of listings with different styles and price ranges. You, however, must defend the architect's floorplans and the builder's reputation.
ADVANTAGE: You can maximize the newness, an insured warranty, the appliances and innovations.
CHALLENGE: You must know everything pertinent about those advantages. Company and product knowledge is critical. You must be a master at overcoming (or minimizing) objections.

POTENTIAL

As a new home sales professional, you are a member of an elite fraternity. For obvious reasons, hardly everyone wants to be a salesperson — of widgets or anything; salespeople have to weather too many emotional and economic storms. Even fewer people get serious about real estate, though many try it. A select group become top-drawer salespeople who can succeed in new home sales.

The good news is that if you can get past the hurdles which obstruct the general working public from entering your profession, it is not only possible for you to survive, but to become wealthy. It's not unusual to get reports from my clients of consistent six-figure incomes.

You can join that select group!

WHICH COMES FIRST — SUCCESS OR CONFIDENCE?

Your success as a new home salesperson hinges on preparation and confidence. Confidence comes from knowledge and expertise. When you know your industry from A to Z, when you know exactly how your homes stack up against the competition, when you know so much about the customer's problems that you are absolutely sure you can render them a genuine, vital service. How can you help not being confident?

The new home salesperson must be prepared to take advantage of *every* opportunity and to meet *every* objection. That *"slight-edge"* professional then faces each prospective buyer with greater confidence than the person who is unwilling to prepare.

A confident attitude breaks down barriers of uncertainty, doubt and disbelief. With these obstacles out of the way, you have a straight road ahead for making a spectacular presentation of your homes' advantages, benefits and your company's services. While the average salesperson simply tries to keep from hindering a new home sale, a successful salesperson *causes* a transaction to happen and knows — every step of the way — what took place.

Success comes to the confident, prepared salesperson, and you can become one of the best!

THE *"SLIGHT-EDGE"*

As you study this book and seek to improve your career, aim high enough to stretch yourself but not so high that you lose hope and give up after a few weeks. Keep your goals practical. Don't become so intent on climbing new home sales mountains that you fail to take the necessary steps to scale the foothills.

Do you want to know one of life's greatest "secrets"? You can be a phenomenal success by being even slightly better than your competition.

"Little things mean a lot" are more than catchy words to a Fifties' Patti Page song. To the top salespeople, those words describe a philosophy of selling that enables them to succeed year after year.

The Kentucky Derby has been won by less than a quarter of an inch; the *"slight-edge"* winner sold for $1,000,000, but the loser only brought $10,000. The Super Bowl Championship has been decided by less than a touchdown. The World Series has been won by one run. The Master's Tournament check has gone to the one-stroke winner in a sudden-death ending.

In 1989, Orel Hershiser shattered baseball salary records by inking a three-year contract worth $7,900,000. On his way to a world championship the previous year, the Los Angeles Dodgers' pitcher kept a portable computer in the dugout which gave *"slight-edge"* information about the batters he would pitch. His intense dedication, superb talent and attention to details helped him win 26 games during the season, and 17 of the games he pitched — including both of his world series outings — were decided by one or two runs.

In 1960, John F. Kennedy defeated Richard M. Nixon by only 113,000 votes, one-half vote per precinct. Political analysts since then point to the crucial television debate when JFK'S tousled hair and warmth edged Nixon's five o'clock shadow and cold demeanor. Kennedy's people had simply done a slightly better job of preparation.

At the end, it is attention to detail that makes all the difference in the world. It's the center fielder's extra two steps to the left, a manager's last-minute product check or a hotel chain's determination to provide "one more" service, such as two Godiva chocolates on the pillow of a turned-down bed.

As a new home salesperson, your professional success will undoubtedly depend on being a percent or two better than the rest. Practice-Drill-Rehearse. That extra-effort, second-mile determination will propel you toward new plateaus of selling success.

Little, apparently insignificant differences between you and your competitors can mean everything. Recognize and capitalize your *"slight- edge."* Where you are slightly better than someone else, use it to your advantage and make it pay off.

Remember, the secret of success for every salesperson who is, or has ever reached the top 5% of our industry, lies in the fact that he or she has developed a penchant for doing things that mediocre salespeople don't like to do.

Although "little things mean a lot" is a simplistic philosophy, you can make the *"slight-edge"* theory work for you and your customers. When you get it working for you, the "lot" will translate into a lot of sales, fulfillment and assets!

The principle differences between the average salesperson and the *"slight-edge"* professional are these:

1. Successful salespeople discipline themselves to do those things which non-successful salespeople refuse to do!!! Such as:
- Controlling their attitude
- Mastering their presentation skills
- Perform diligent, thorough and consistent *"follow-through"*
- Being serious goal setters and masters of time management
- Constantly seeking new information about their craft
- Doing everything with sincerity, honesty and integrity

2. The average salesperson simply engages in a conversation with the customer until the customer is ready to conclude it. However, the professional has an organized and planned presentation which they control, while at all times it is conversational. The presentation is not a social event. It is a business event in which we must be sociable.

3. The average salesperson will not stand in the way of a transaction taking place. However, the professional causes it to happen and knows every step of the way what they did, how they did it and why they did it.

OPPORTUNITY

One thing that distresses me as I travel throughout this country is the fact that we are surrounded by so many opportunities that we become blinded and jaded to them.

So many people have reached a comfort level, for whatever reason, and have lost the battle to mediocrity. I was like that. I worked in a real estate office while attending college, and I realized very quickly that there was a lot of money to be made in selling real estate. Soon afterwards I discovered the potential in new home sales. I began with Florida's largest volume home builder, a wet-behind-the-ears addition to a sales staff of 35 people. Within months I became their top salesperson. Three years later I was named vice-president of sales and marketing for that company. Later I moved on to the presidency of a corporation which was involved in development, marketing and management of planned communities throughout Florida.

But I hit a period of time when I was complacent. Instead of excelling, I was content to be mediocre, to merely get by.

Now that I have matured, I realize that being the "best" for me often meant that I was the best of the worst — judging my success by the failures of others.

A few years ago I learned a life-changing lesson. As consultant to the Jack Nicklaus Development Corporation, I got to be around one of history's greatest golfers and athletes. In preparation for the seminar we were to do, I did some reading and research and was told that he had been quoted once in an interview as saying:

> "I have won some tournaments, received the trophies and checks for winning, but there were championships that I really didn't feel that I really won. Sure, the press said that I came in first place, but I didn't play as well as I know I could have and the other people didn't either."

Isn't that interesting? He came in first, but in his mind he didn't win. You see, Jack Nicklaus is a consummate, *"slight-edge"* professional." He plays against himself. He competes against "The Jack Nicklaus Standard."

What about you? In the greatest, most bountiful nation that has ever existed, what are you doing to make a difference? What are you doing with your God-given talents? Are you making the most of your opportunities,

or are you — as I discovered I was — content to be upper-mediocre?
You can become the best of the best in new home sales. **Go for it!**

1. There is nothing quite like being a new home salesperson.

2. As a new home salesperson, you face a rapidly changing marketplace.

3. As a new home salesperson, you face at least six hurdles which existing home salespeople don't encounter.

4. As a new home sales professional, you are a member of an elite fraternity; plus, you have an enviable potential to be highly-paid professional.

5. Your success as a new home salesperson hinges on preparation and confidence.

Chapter Two

THE CUSTOMER BUYS YOU FIRST

". . .nothing in life just happens. It isn't enough to believe in something; you have to have the stamina to meet obstacles and overcome them, to struggle."[1]

—GOLDA MEIR, Former Prime Minister of Israel[1]

LET'S START AT THE BEGINNING

What separates great new home salespeople from the average ones? For starters, let me destroy some illusions:

MYTH: Great salespeople are naturally genial and communicative.

TRUTH: Salespeople are made, not born. The best ones have often overcome mental or physical stumbling-blocks — timidity, stuttering, shyness and lack of education.

MYTH: Selling is a game of subterfuge and competition, so the prime money is made by slick, fast-talking con artists.

TRUTH: Maybe selling used to be a haven for snake-oil peddlers and swampland purveyors, but today's successful salespeople, with well-publicized exceptions, are the proverbial cream of the crop, in terms of value-added service and quality-mindedness.

MYTH: Great salespeople are thick-skinned. They were born without a fear of rejection.

TRUTH: I have yet to meet a sales professional who doesn't agonize over missed sales, failed customers and lackluster presentations.

MYTH: All great salespeople are merciless debaters and hard closers.

TRUTH: Try the ultra-hard close in new home sales and the prospect will walk out on you! This business requires an extraordinary amount of savvy, common sense and tact. Genuine professionalism is more than a trite phrase in this industry.

MYTH: Selling new homes is war, and the best salespeople are seasoned, scarred combat veterans who have learned how to outwit, dislodge and overwhelm opponents.

TRUTH: Ditto the previous TRUTH!

---

1. Golda Meir, My Life (New York: Putnam, 1975), p. 26.

SALESPERSON!

The mere word conjures up a number of negative meanings.

Let me ask you: What is the first word that pops into your mind when you hear "SALESPERSON?"

With audiences of all numbers, I've done association games with that term. The same synonyms keep coming up:

"Slick."

"Pushy."

"Used cars."

"Overbearing."

"Sleazy."

"Dislike."

"Con artist."

Research shows that more than 90% of the American buying public has a conscious/subconscious disdain for salespeople. This is partly due to the image — fairly or unfairly — which has been created by experience or painted by certain segments of the media.

Much of the responsibility for this pervasive attitude must be placed on the shoulders of a great number of salespeople.

Everyone, it seems, has a ready collection of "war stories" with stereotypically rude or apathetic salespeople. Let me share three personal samples:

DON had no idea who I was when he met me at the door of his company's model home. I often pose as a customer as I prepare for an upcoming sales seminar.

Don asked, "May I help you?" (Strike one!)

"No thanks," I answered; "I'm just looking."

"Oh," he pouted, obviously disappointed. (Strike two!)

"Could I have some information about your model homes," I posed.

"We've got some great looking brochures," he bragged, "but we just ran out. If you'll hang on for a few minutes, I'll go to the sales office and see if I can rustle up one for you." (Out!)

** **ELAINE'S** greeting was friendly enough when I walked into her company's real estate sales office near my home (checking out the competition). She remained seated behind her desk and asked me to register. Then she assured me that a salesperson would be with me momentarily.

She was the only person in sight, and was less interested in my business than in smoking a cigarette, drinking a Coke and watching General Hospital (at the same time — what coordination!).

**** The situations are real, but the names have been changed.**

There were three other customers there, drinking coffee and looking at wall displays of floorplans, and they shrugged as if to underscore the curious situation.

When I pointedly asked her a question about one of the floorplans, she looked at me blankly and said, "That's not really in my department, but the sales manager will be back in a minute from Burger Boy. Can you hold on until then?"

I waited a minute then walked out. Elaine didn't even notice; she was glued to one of the TV monitors.

KURT, a receptionist for a new home sales company in the Midwest, made it clear from the time he answered the telephone that I was an interruption in his day. As I asked him several pointed questions, he was efficient in his duties, but it was clear that his mind was elsewhere.

I couldn't restrain myself from doing a bit of research. That was a mistake. When I asked him if there was something wrong, he spent the next 10 minutes generally running down the "Mickey Mouse" company he worked for, with the "inept" salespeople as specific targets.

You could tell me your own stories about the arrogant, petty, untrained, disorganized, overbearing, obviously lying salespeople with whom you come in contact. These things should never happen — not if you want to be a professional in our industry.

YOUR FIRST TASK — SELL YOURSELF ON SELLING

Because selling is not respected, for reasons already mentioned, even top-flight salespeople tend to become defensive about the way they earn their living. As a consequence, many high calibre salespeople fail to live up to their potential and eventually leave the sales profession altogether.

That is sad, because selling, of all the professions, should be the most respected.

Selling, despite the "bad apples" in our industry, is absolutely crucial to our society. Nothing happens until somebody sells something to someone. Selling is the lifeblood of a healthy economy.

Every job in the private sector is underpinned by sales. The inventors, the engineers who design products, the production workers who turn raw materials into finished goods, the accountants who keep track of the numbers, the clerical people who work in the office, the truck drivers who take the products to the retailer and the managers throughout the company. All are dependent on the salespeople.

Translate that into new home sales: If you do not come through with sales, your company will not have the revenues necessary to pay salaries, to buy raw materials or to pay land costs. From this perspective, the sales-

---

** **The situations are real, but the names have been changed.**

person is vital to the welfare of all other employees in the company. Carry the thought a step further (suppliers, construction workers, raw material producers, draftspeople . . .), and you can see just how important you are!

Selling is about solving problems, clarifying perceptions and advocating positions. A good salesperson educates the customer and helps them solve real problems while advocating the value of a particular product or service. The good salesperson serves his or her own interests by putting the customer's best interests first. When this happens throughout the marketplace, the economy flourishes.

You are *very* important!

THE ALPHABET OF NEW HOME SALES SUCCESS

Because you are so vitally important to the process, you must be totally prepared to perform at all times.

Think about this — the average builder invests (or spends) between $100 to as much as $700 or more to bring *each customer* through the door of your sales office. That means that you, the professional representative of your company, have an awesome opportunity (and responsibility).

What kind of person succeeds in new home sales? I have worked with thousands of new home salespeople, and the finest, most prosperous ones share 26 most-likely-to-succeed attributes. To be a professional new home salesperson, *A to Z*, you must be. . .

Aware

The professional who is aware is better able to communicate with people. Awareness provides a powerful edge over complacent competition.

Read the *Wall Street Journal* every morning. Devour anything you can find on sales, positive thinking, market trends and real estate. As a real estate professional, you should scan the *Nation's Building News* (published by the National Association of Home Builders), *Real Estate Today* (published by the National Association of Realtors) and your local newspaper.

Also, if you are involved in a specialized type of product, you should be aware of trends and events in your niche. For example, if your company markets to a high percentage of retirees, you should be reading such periodicals as *Golden Years* and *Modern Maturity.*

If you want to be recognized as a professional, then be professional! Keep abreast of your market. Develop a keen insight into the attitudes of the people with whom you are dealing. Be aware!

Believable

To be successful, you must persuade. To persuade, you must educate. To educate, you must be believable.

There are enough salespeople out there who are content to "wing it." Be different. Know your sales presentation so well that you can say it with confidence and poise.

Believability is a strength born through extensive mental rehearsal.

Consistent

I believe that anyone can sell new homes. When the market is flourishing, a person can be mediocre, have bad habits — and *still* look good.

Your challenge is to constantly improve your speaking, writing and listening skills.

Zig Ziglar often says, "Never judge your success based upon the failures of other people."

Just because you are making sales doesn't mean that you are successful. Even being the top salesperson in your company does not necessarily mean that you are the best. It could mean that you are the best of the worst.

Instead, judge your success based upon this question: "Am I *consistently* doing the very best I can with the talent I have?"

Consistency is one of the most important character traits needed by a new home sales professional.

Determined

A determined professional possesses a rare combination of rugged independence and organizational esprit de corps. He or she seems to have an innate ability to make things happen.

Be tenacious in achieving your goals. Be committed to do your best. Put negative influences and missed sales aside.

Enthusiastic

The last four letters of the word "enthusiasm" explain everything:

I
A*m*
S*old*
M*yself*

Sell yourself first — on your purpose in life, your family, your country, your company and your product. Once you are sold, you will have no trouble being enthusiastic.

Remember, the top professionals have an ability to make things happen. Why? Enthusiasm!

Flexible

Most of us tend to get set in our ways. The best in any field of endeavor, however, keep looking for that *"slight-edge"* way to do something better.

Don't change merely for change's sake, but develop a willingness to change. Learn to recognize new advances and innovations; this will keep you ahead of the pack.

Goal-oriented

You must have an idea where you want to be and how you are going to get there. More to the point: If you fail to plan, you plan to fail.

Be astute in your goal-setting prowess. Always write your goals (If you don't write a goal down, you are still in a wishful-thinking mode!). Cultivate a seasoned capacity for constantly upgrading your short-, medium- and long-range goals.

Wrote Robert Browning, "A man's reach should exceed his grasp, or what's a heaven for?"

Honest

People should be able to count on you, to believe in you. In virtually every corporate and marketplace survey of desired characteristics, integrity is the highest-rated.

To achieve long-term success in this business, you have to be honest and possess a record of living up to your commitments.

Beyond that point, an honest salesperson never, ever is afraid to close someone. Why? When the closing is based on honest facts and principles, that sales professional who has built a bridge of honesty recognizes that the sale is more for the customer's benefit than for personal gain.

Inquisitive

Creativity and ability to innovate comes from asking lots of "What if.. ?" and "I wonder if there's a better way. . . ?" questions.

A great salesperson asks a number of questions in the sales presentation, constantly probing for information and feedback.

To succeed in new home sales, allow your mind to be genuinely inquisitive.

Judicious

Defined as having, applying or showing sound wisdom, this word's root is "judge."

How does this apply to new home sales? The pressure is on! Can you be wise, careful and discreet even when the heat is on?

Knowledgeable

Be a problem-solver. Start by being more knowledgeable about your product than your co-workers. Prepare yourself by becoming more familiar with your competitors' product than your competitors are.

Loyal

If you haven't already established a reputation for rock-hard, 100% loyalty, you will be haunted by this defect for the rest of your career.

A reputation for disloyalty is bound to make you unwelcome anywhere in new home sales. You make your way to the top not by back-stabbing, but by establishing early on in your career an unshakable reputation as a true, stand-up professional.

Motivated

Nido Qubein, the best-selling author and top-flight corporate consultant says, "When you become a professional, you give up the right to think negative, to talk negative and to be negative."

Whatever else you are, you must be a highly motivated professional with optimum self-esteem and a tremendously positive attitude.

Here's one of my secrets: Learn to use the word "incredible".

When someone asks, "How's business?" Answer, "It's incredible!" If you just closed three houses in the past two hours, or if you haven't sold a home in a month, you can honestly say, "It's incredible!"

Get in the habit of saying that word to yourself and others. You will be programming yourself for success. You will become more self-motivated.

Neat

You have to be extra-careful in this area. People want to buy new homes from professionals who are neat in appearance, dress, hygiene and demeanor. Your automobile should be the cleanest in the parking lot.

And you should never smoke in a customer's presence. I could retire on the commissions lost by associates and clients whose customers were turned off by either a lighted cigarette or by the overpowering smell which lingers around a smoker.

If you must smoke, either light up off duty or prepare to live on a limited income. (Incidently, not smoking may also improve your physical as well as financial health).

Organized

Do you keep "To Do" lists? Does your desk, calendar, notebook and automobile reflect the kind of salesperson with whom you would like to do business?

Don't always be ruled by the urgent and immediate. Don't let poor planning cause an endless series of "emergencies."

Focus on the most important priorities, and develop a system for getting your life in order. The increased sales will pay off handsomely.

Prepared

Do your homework better than anyone else. Know what you are going to do at all times. Practice, Drill and Rehearse! Role-play. Become quick on your feet by being prepared.

Quick to learn

John H. Johnson, Founder of Johnson Publishing Company (*Ebony, Jet,* and *Black World*), CEO of Supreme Life Insurance Company, and President of Fashion Fair Cosmetics was asked, "How do you recognize a good potential employee?"

He responded:

> "By observing. I look for dedication and commitment, and willingness to learn. I think it's more the last than it is anything else, because an intelligent person can be taught almost anything that's not purely technical. So we look primarily for a desire to learn and a dedication to the job. If they have these, we can teach them the rest."[2]

One of my favorite quotes is, "It's what we learn after we know it all that really counts."

Resilient

The sales professional is the only line of work, with the possible exception of boxing and football, in which a person gets paid to take abuse.

You discover what you have inside when you make a great presentation and the "friendly" couple suddenly begin dumping on you: "We don't like your company. We don't like your houses. Furthermore, we don't like you."

Anthony Robbins, in *Unlimited Power*, writes:

> "Winners, leaders, masters — people with personal power — all understand that if you try something and do not get the outcome you want, it's simply feedback. You use that information to make finer distinctions about what you need to do to produce the results you desire."[3]

Sometimes determination means that you have to say, as the almost-beaten Rocky character declared, "I ain't goin' down any more!"

Single-minded in purpose

How focused or centered are you on becoming the best new home sales-person you can be?

Before you begin any presentation, you should reaffirm your mission by asking yourself these three questions:

"Who am I?"

"Where am I?"

"Why am I here?"

Unless you can focus yourself during every presentation, you may have a problem developing a life-long single-mindedness of purpose. Other-wise, you will be continually drawn off course. (The better often keeps us from the best.)

Time conscious

Time is a non-replenishable natural resource. The success you enjoy tomorrow will be in direct proportion to your ability to manage time today.

The top new home sales professionals understand the importance of

---

2. Harvard Business Review, March-April 1976, p. 124.
3. Anthony Robbins, Unlimited Power (New York: Fawcett, 1986), p.74.

doing weekly planners — listing the activities that they must accomplish in the week, then breaking those down into daily and hourly activities.

I have noticed that the best-paid veterans realize that one of the keys to time-management is to spend the first hours of each working day doing the most difficult things.

Success hinges on your ability to maximize your time!

Understanding

LuAnn Sullivan, a manager with the Wells Fargo Bank, said this time-proven truth:

> "If you don't show your appreciation to your people, then they're going to stop caring, and then you are going to find yourself out of business."

Translate that into your life as a new home salesperson. Be empathetic with your customers. Understand why things can't always be exactly the way you want them to be. Feel the needs of other people.

Vibrant

Develop a love for life. Your attitude, after all, is a choice that you make. You can look at everything as the worst thing that could have happened to you, or you can say, "That's the greatest thing that could have happened to me."

Love what you are doing. Like people. Your attitude will translate into mega-bucks because people enjoy doing business with vibrant salespeople.

Wealth-minded

Wealth means so much more than having a fat wallet and enviable assets. There are people who don't have a lot money who are very wealthy. Conversely, there are people who have seven-figure and eight-figure bank balances but are mentally impoverished.

Be wealth-minded — mentally, physically, spiritually, professionally — and financial wealth will be the natural reward.

X-traordinary

Ordinary people do things in ordinary ways. Extraordinary people do things in *extra*ordinary ways.

Develop your own style. Be memorable. Use your talents and blend them with a little bit of showbiz.

The best new home sales professionals have a talent for making an impact on the opinions and actions of others — an influence so subtle that it may go unrecognized at first.

You-oriented

Some call the past decade the "ME Generation." As we move into the twenty-first century, I believe we will see a curious blend of pragmatic selfishness and service-oriented selflessness. For the real estate professional, the trend must be centered on value-added quality.

Certainly, you are important, but so is everyone else. As a professional, you must learn to put your own wants aside so that you can identify your customer's needs.

Earl Nightingale said, "If you help enough people to get what they want, you will automatically get what you want."

Develop a genuine interest in people. Otherwise, even if you have the combined acting talent of Dustin Hoffman and Meryl Streep, the customers will see through your facade.

Zealous

The best salespeople are driven by a sense of mission. What is important to you? What are you willing to do in order to reach your goals?

Foster an ardent interest in the pursuit of the things that you feel are most worthwhile. Resolve to be zealous about setting priorities for your career and your life.

The difference between interest and commitment is that when you only have interest in something, you do what it takes only when it's convenient, but when you have commitment, you accept no excuses, just results.

HOW DO YOU RATE — A TO Z?

Identify your own sales professional profile, using the *Alphabet of Success*. Rate your characteristics using the following numbers:

5 (always)
4 (most of the time)
3 (half and half)
2 (seldom)
1 (never)

_____ AWARE	_____ NEAT
_____ BELIEVABLE	_____ ORGANIZED
_____ CONSISTENT	_____ PREPARED
_____ DETERMINED	_____ QUICK TO LEARN
_____ ENTHUSIASTIC	_____ RESILIENT
_____ FLEXIBLE	_____ SINGLE-MINDED OF PURPOSE
_____ GOAL-ORIENTED	_____ TIME-CONSCIOUS
_____ HONEST	_____ UNDERSTANDING
_____ INQUISITIVE	_____ VIBRANT
_____ JUDICIOUS	_____ WEALTH-MINDED
_____ KNOWLEDGEABLE	_____ X-TRAORDINARY
_____ LOYAL	_____ YOU-ORIENTED
_____ MOTIVATED	_____ ZEALOUS

SCORING:

59 or less	MAJOR CORRECTIONS ARE CRITICAL.
60-89	AREAS OF IMPROVEMENT ARE ESSENTIAL.
90-109	SOME PROGRESS SHOULD BE DESIRED.
110-130	WOW!

ANALYZE YOUR SCORE: Determine your weakest areas, then develop a plan of action and write specific goals as to how you are going to improve those characteristics.

A FINAL NOTE

From A to Z, success in new home sales takes uncommon commitment, dedication, study, practice and persistence. No faint-hearted types need apply!

Since the remainder of *THE OFFICIAL HANDBOOK FOR NEW HOME SALESPEOPLE* centers on helping you reach the top 5% of your profession, make a mental note to re-take this Alphabet of Success quiz after completing the book. You may be surprised at the improved results!

1. The customer buys YOU first!
2. Selling, of all the professions, should be the most respected.
3. Because you are so vitally important to society and the economy, you must be totally prepared to perform at all times.
4. Success in new home sales takes an uncommon commitment — from A to Z!

Chapter Three

HOW TO POSITION YOURSELF FOR NEW HOME SALES SUCCESS

"What you are speaks so loudly that I cannot hear what you say."

—RALPH WALDO EMERSON
American Essayist and Poet

PRIMARILY, YOU ARE *NOT* A NEW HOME SALESPERSON

After spending previous chapters explaining several basics of being a great new home salesperson, let me offer this paradoxical statement:

Your primary responsibility is not to sell new homes. . .FIRST AND FOREMOST, YOU ARE A PROFESSIONAL COMMUNICATOR!

Until you realize and maximize your first responsibility, you relegate yourself to being less than your best.

Everything you do — what you wear, say, think, demonstrate, confer, suggest and represent — must be directed toward becoming a master communicator. When you position yourself as a championship communicator, your new home sales career will skyrocket!

Subsequent chapters will deal with specific areas of sales communications. In this chapter I want to present several vital foundations for positioning yourself as a master communicator.

WHAT IS POSITIONING?

Positioning, in a sentence, means breaking through a prospective customer's barricades, while maximizing his or her reasons for buying from you. Piercing a prospect's blockades depends more upon your *"slight- edge"* than on your force, talent, finesse or technique.

I talked about the *"slight-edge"* approach to selling before, mentioning the 5% advantage. Let me offer another example, narrowing that edge to 3%.

A few years ago, a racehorse named Achmed became one of the first horses in history to win more than $1 million in a single season. During that same season, there was another horse which came in second in almost every race Achmed won.

Interestingly, Achmed won 15 times as much money as the horse which consistently came in second. Later, the champion was sold for 10 times more money than the second runner.

Does that mean that Achmed was 15 times faster than his nearest competitor? That question intrigued a sportswriter, so he made a study of the times logged by the two horses. Achmed's finishing times averaged only 3% faster than the slower horse.

Simply stated, the champion that year had a winner's edge of only 3% over his nearest competitor, but it was enough to bring his owner 15 times more prize money and give him 10 times as much value.

The ability to gain and hold the attention of enough of the right people gives the top 5% of salespeople their edge. Develop your *"slight-edge"* with these five points:

1. **Position yourself one notch above your competition.**
   Dress slightly better, carry a more impressive briefcase and express yourself more effectively.
   Jim, a client and friend, has become a true believer when it comes to the positioning edge of dressing for success. In the past few years he has moved up from $99 off-the-rack polyester bargains to $700-plus Giorgio Armani suits. When Jim talks about the first time he put the suit on, he says, "It was like a bolt of self-confidence. I thought I was already very positive, motivated and enthusiastic, but I swear when I put that suit on, I walked and talked differently."
   Now, you don't have to rush out and mortgage the farm to be able to buy $700 plus suits. Success does not require a Giorgio Armani (nor can a suit guarantee success!), but you must find a way to be one notch better than your competition in your attire, tools-of-the-trade and expression.
   The image you project does affect the way you feel and act. It also affects the way others respond to you.

2. **Make a great first impression.**
   What is your initial perception of anyone you meet? It's how he or she comes across to you *visually*.
   First impressions do count. According to a recent survey in *USA Today*, 21% of corporate interviewers make a hiring decision in the first one-to-five minutes of a job candidate's initial interview, and nearly half of the hiring decisions are made within 10 minutes.
   The percentages run even higher for new home sales. You must position yourself for maximum impact during those first seconds.
   How?

   - Create a confident manner(not superior, condescending nor inferior).
   - Present a clean, neat appearance.
   - Be well-groomed and reasonably conservative in taste.
   - Smile!
   - Speak in a pleasant manner.
   - Use the prospect's name and pronounce it correctly.
   - Never apologize for taking your prospect's time.
   - Never be rude or careless.

   The object of the first few seconds of the sales interview is to get favorable attention. Anyone can get noticed with flamboyancy and obnoxious behavior, but favorable recognition, the kind that leads to sales success, takes careful consideration of positioning details.

3. **Position yourself as an expert whom your prospects, customers and Realtors can take seriously.**

   Know your market better than the rest, and establish yourself as the best new home salesperson with which any prospect or Realtor can work.

   Present yourself as a sales expert, a design connoisseur, a financing specialist, and a competent guide to all new home dreams.

   Make sure that you are suitably attired for the atmosphere your company has created. Neither overdress nor dress so carelessly that it might look as if you do not value the role you play as a new home sales representative.

   Pay careful attention to the kind of pen you use, to your shoes, and to your hair (especially when it is windy and you have to go outside a lot).

   Positioning yourself as an expert means balancing outward and inward professionalism.

4. **Position yourself as one who has a burning desire to serve your customers exceptionally well.**

   Don't try to fake this. Your customers will see through you in a New York minute. If you can't cultivate a genuine interest in the needs of your customers, you are in the wrong business.

5. **Make the customer feel important.**

   Never, ever let them think that you have anything more important to do than to be with them at that moment.

   Become a world champion at quickly establishing common ground with your customers. Do this by asking questions.

   The more common ground you have, the more likely they will open up with you. The more they communicate with you, the more likely they will listen and agree with your presentation.

   Does positioning work? Consider the fact that the top 5% of salespeople close more than one-fourth all the sales they attempt. Why? They have learned the secret of positioning.

   Positioning yourself in the top 5% provides that extra edge for piercing resistance and maximizing your sales efforts, but it requires a top-flight attitude and singleness of purpose!

TEN POSITIONING MINDSETS OF A NEW HOME SALES PROFESSIONAL

During my years as a new home salesperson, manager, consultant and educator, I have noticed that the *"slight-edge"* veterans seem to have superior mindsets. A mindset is something that a person does without thinking about it. A mindset is automatic, practiced and natural.

Here are 10 specific mindsets that are absolutely crucial to the person who wants to be a top professional in this business.

1. **Before making *any* presentation, I will ask myself these three questions:**

   "Who am I?" (Give a few words that describe where you fit in the selling process.)
   "Where am I?" (Specifically?)
   "What am I here to accomplish?" (Your top priority?)

   One of the most succinct answers a seminar participant gave to these questions was:

   "I am a professional, in my arena, to win!"

   I have already mentioned these questions, and the primary reason for establishing them as a mindset is to help you focus all your energies on the "Main Event" facing you.

   Many things happen during the course of a day to interrupt and fragment you. If someone walks through the door and you are not ready to perform, it may cost your company $100 to $700 or more!!

   Stop throwing that money away! Instead, develop your three-to-five second positioning mindset.

2. **I will never assume *anything* but the sale.**

   If I don't try, they won't buy! Yet how many times do salespeople quit before they even start, because they predetermine, by judging a person's clothing or automobile, that a person isn't going to buy?

   This is one of my own war stories: During the early 70s I was involved in a first-time homebuyer program in Florida. The homes ranged from $30,000 to $50,000. We had six salespeople on our team.

   It was the middle of the week and the prospect-flow had been very slow. We worked on a first in/first out rotation system. I was fifth in line, and by four in the afternoon only four prospects had come through the doors.

   I knew that it was my "up," ("Cancel- Cancel") and I glanced out the sales office window just in time to see a young couple drive up in an old, beat-up car. They got out of the car and spent a few moments looking around. They weren't nicely dressed. In short, they didn't fit my ideal buyers' profile.

I didn't want to waste my "up" ("Cancel-Cancel") on them, so I took a step over to Jim, the salesman who was in line behind me. He hadn't seen the prospects yet.

"Jim" I said, "I'm kind of bored. I want to go walk around through the models, so if anyone comes in, why don't we trade places. You take the next one, and I'll take the one after yours. Okay?"

Jim thought it was a good deal, since he was wondering if Prospect Number Six would even show up that afternoon.

I left, gloating at the fast one I'd put over on Jim. Perhaps fifteen minutes later, I came walking back in. Jim was sitting at his desk filling in the blanks on a purchase agreement. The seedy-looking man was writing out a check.

I was bewildered. Because I was one of the best salespeople in the company, I thought I had a real estate version of ESP. I thought I could take one look and tell who the buyers were.

After the people left, I asked Jim, "What's going on?"

"Bob," he shot back, "you won't believe this. It's the darnedest thing I've ever seen. That couple walked in the door right after you left, and one of the very first questions they asked was: `We've only saved $15,000. . .is that enough to be able to buy one of your new homes?' Within a few minutes, as you saw, they were writing out their check."

The check went through. The sale was finalized shortly afterward. Within weeks, that couple's home was being built.

They had been saving their money to buy a new home, and had been willing to get by with the clothing and automobile they owned until they got into their new home.

The mistake I made that day cost me $1500, but it was a cheap education considering the many thousands of dollars that I have received since because I learned a very, very valuable lesson.

Never assume anything but the sale!

3. **I will always be prepared and have an organized, planned, conversational presentation.**

   In order to be organized and prepared, you will master the *FIVE-MINUTE PRESENTATION* (Chapter Nine).

   You will then know the features and benefits, and you will be able to convey them with emotional impact (Chapters Nine, Ten and Eleven). You will know in advance the objections that you are likely to receive (Chapter Twelve) and will have Practiced, Drilled and Rehearsed (PDR) every logical, plausible and understandable answer.

4. **My primary job as a master communicator in the presentation process is to constantly seek the truth. You seek the truth by probing, asking questions and using involvement selling skills.**

5. **I will qualify everyone using the C.O.M.M.A. qualifying approach.**
   You can use this acronym to remember the basic elements that you wish to know — as soon as possible — about the prospect:

   C*ommitment*
   O*pportunity*
   M*oney*
   M*otivation*
   A*ction*

   I will be teaching more about the C.O.M.M.A. qualifying approach during subsequent chapters.

6. **When necessary, I will answer a question with a question.**
   You need to know why they are asking the question, plus you can use this technique to get the prospect more involved in the selling process.

7. **I will skillfully use appropriate involvement questions and tie-down statements throughout my presentation.**
   Tie-downs (involvement questions) will cause people to own the concept that you've given them, especially when they answer your tie-downs affirmatively.

8. **In every presentation I will ask for the sale at least three times.**
   Anything less casts doubt on your commitment to the selling profession and disregards potential customers' needs. It also brings out their objections.

9. **I will handle objections by skillfully using the "6 Step Method".**

10. **Whenever I ask a closing question, I will shut up!**
    I will be quiet for one major reason: Whoever talks next owns it.

    When the prospect has shown interest and can afford the home, if he or she does not buy after I have made a presentation, I must accept the responsibility.
    You didn't explain the opportunity correctly, or they did not believe you. Either way, both you and the prospect lose.

A FINAL WORD

If your attitudes and actions do not stimulate your potential buyers in positive ways, then you will probably fail in your larger goal of motivating them to own your new home.

Remember, anyone can sell homes when the market is good. People are going to buy a place to live, regardless of your professionalism (or lack of it!). The secret to *"slight-edge"* success is becoming great at closing the "impossible" prospects whom others cannot close.

Make the most of your opportunities by positioning yourself for new home sales success. Your role is to create a climate of trust and confidence while presenting the basic facts about your homes.

Never forget that everything centers on your communication mastery and sales savvy. No one gets paid until something is sold!

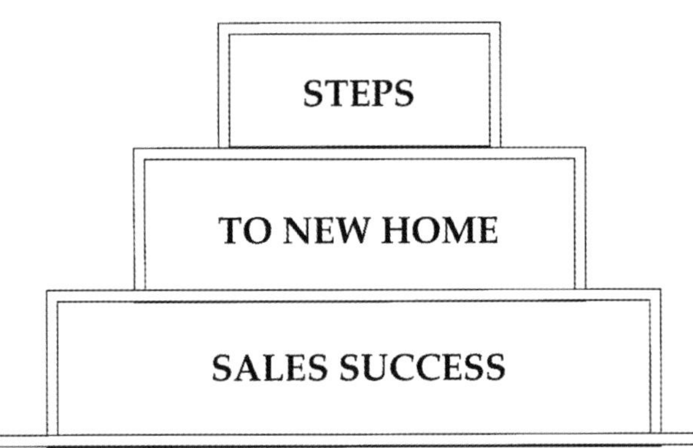

1. You are not a new home salesperson; first and foremost, you are a professional communicator.
2. First impressions of you can either be valuable or expensive.
3. Position yourself for *"slight-edge"* success.
4. Develop the 10 position Mindsets of a new home sales professional.

SECTION II
UNDERSTANDING THE CUSTOMER

Chapter Four

HOW TO QUALIFY PLENTY OF CUSTOMERS

"It's better to have a philosophy to out-think your competition than to outspend them." —LES WOLFF [1]

UNDERSTANDING SALES BASICS

Selling new homes can be the easiest, most simple job in the world if you work it smart, but it will be the hardest, most complicated job in the world if you try to work it wrong.

Here are four bottom-lines to remember:

1. You cannot collect hefty commissions until you close lots of sales.
2. You cannot close lots of sales until you write a number of purchase agreements.
3. You cannot write a number of purchase agreements until you conduct many successful interviews.
4. You cannot have many successful interviews without coming face to face with lots of qualified prospects.

There, in a nutshell is the foundation of the business of selling new homes — you must come face to face with lots of qualified prospects and have a quality presentation.

PROSPECTS

I have found that 20% of all real estate people, those who sell both new and existing homes, make 80% of all the real estate sales. Other surveys and sales statistics confirm my research.

To put this set of statistics more succinctly, 80% of the salespeople are left to fight over the remaining 20% of business.

Your goal is to discover how to work smart — to find a way into the top 20%. Ultimately, your goal should be to move into the top 5% who have as high as a 50% presentation-to-closing ratio.

In my observations, the lower 80% of salespeople, those who grapple over the leftover 20% of customers, do so for one major reason: Most of them rely on their eight-hour-a-day "model home time" to provide all their interview leads.

"But I am in new home sales!" you argue. "It's my company's job to bring the prospects through the door, and it's my job to be courteous, hand out

---

1. Roger von Oech, Ph. D., A Whack on the Side of the Head, (New York: Warner, 1983), p. 43.

brochures, answer questions and provide information. If a prospect indicates interest in a specific house, then it's my job to sell them a home."

True. You cannot be expected to invest thousands of dollars in advertising and merchandising. It's the job of your company to provide an "attraction package" of advertising, telephones, public relations, brochures, business cards and marketing helps.

You are absolutely correct with the "It's-my-company's-job" answer, but if you live by that motto, you also relegate yourself to a lower income.

Are you interested in beginning the trek toward the top 20% or 5%? If so, you have to be much more than a glorified order-taker. You must find creative ways to make more presentations, and must make those presentations memorable!

DON'T MISS GOOD PROSPECTS

First things first. Studies made on why salespeople have problems getting enough prospects to listen to a sales presentation boil down to these three brutal revelations of the deficiencies in the poor-to-average salesperson:

1. **The salesperson doesn't recognize the prospect opportunities surrounding him or her.**

2. **He or she doesn't know where to find an abundance of prospects or is unwilling to develop creative approaches.**

3. **The salesperson is too lazy to look beyond the "normal" flow of prospects.**

I don't know what to do about the third group. As a manager, my primary solution for lazy salespeople is to encourage them to seek another way to make a living.

Let's go to the initial two reasons.

First, every salesperson, even the best, passes by good prospects now and then without recognizing them. Awareness is the key, and that can be developed. Remember, never assume anything but the sale.

Second, don't rely on your "model home time" to provide all of your prospects. We've all been there, haven't we? We sit inside the model office, playing solitaire, making paper airplanes, smoking cigarettes, listening to the game and watching the driveway.

Pity the poor person who still believes that prospects are the exclusive responsibility of the home builder or the advertising agency or someone else. By relying solely on the people who drop-in or phone for interviews, you have given up much of the control of your sales production.

Certainly, as long as the market is good, your company's marketing techniques are working wonders and you are swamped with prospects, you don't have to look for creative ways to develop new prospects. But what happens when you don't have the ideal situation?

Top salespeople find a way to make things happen even when conditions are lousy!

GETTING THE NUMBERS

Effective prospecting begins by figuring your current presentation-to-close ratio. Certainly you will improve your percentages as I teach you to make more effective "Main Event" presentations, to overcome objections quickly and to close with greater finesse.

Calculate your presentation-to-close ratio, then determine X-number of presentations you will need to make to meet your goals. Beyond that, based on your observations, how many warm bodies do you need to face in order to make X-number of presentations? Call the warm bodies your Y-number.

The next question: In your current model home situation, are you "up" — face to face — with enough Y-number warm bodies? If not, dear salesperson, you have a choice. You can sit around wondering why "nothing is shaking," or you can find a way to make things happen.

CREATIVE PLACES TO FIND PROSPECTS

Fortunately, you can develop a positive program for prospecting. Every new home sales company has its own prospecting guidelines and codes. Check with your sales manager before proceeding with any of the following recommendations.

Let me offer seven simple suggestions for finding lots of prospects. Every idea may not work in your situation, but you will undoubtedly find several techniques which will boost your sales production. The secret is to find a way to develop new prospects whether or not they are beating a path to your model home.

1. **Be involved in your community.**

   Position yourself, not as a fly-by-night con artist intent on grabbing commission checks and running, but as a professional real estate salesperson who is interested in the betterment of your community.

   Get involved and be recognized as a solid, stand-up citizen, not merely because it is good business, but because it is great for your personal growth.

   You have plenty of groups and causes available — churches and civic organizations, charities and sporting clubs.

2. **Be alert to new home buying situations.**

   New company start-ups, existing business expansions, corporate mergers — all signal the potential influx of home buyers.

   Make a friendly call to the personnel manager. Offer to be a resource for any real estate questions for the incoming personnel. Leave a stack of business cards and/or brochures.

3. **Check with personnel offices of area companies.**

   In addition to being aware of major influxes of new corporate employees coming into the area, you should maintain contact with personnel offices. Good human resources people can be a good source of leads for individual incoming workers or executives.

   Get creative. If the personnel manager is friendly, show up with doughnuts and coffee someday. Chat for a moment and leave.

   Don't sell anything on these goodwill missions. Just smile and let the people know that you consider them an important part of the community. Leave several of your cards.

   Remember, position yourself as a resource person, not a nuisance.

4. **Cultivate a network of "bird dogs."**

   "Bird dogs" are simply family members, friends or acquaintances who remember to mention your name when the subject of home buying comes up in a conversation. This is probably one of your most untapped sources for new prospects, and the network is directly tied to your community involvement.

   Remember, people won't help you unless they realize that you want help, and unless they know specifically what kind of help you want.

   When you do network with a "bird dog," cultivate that relationship by keeping your source informed of positive developments.

   When the tip results in a sale, you don't necessarily have to pay (and in many states it is illegal) part of your commission, but you should purchase an appropriate gift or take the person to an expensive dinner. Heartfelt thank-you's will undoubtedly result in greater sales production.

5. **Contact your local chamber of commerce.**

   Consider the fact that every year, one out of every five families will move. Moreover, every five years, three out of every five families will move. Many people who are planning a move to your area will contact your chamber of commerce.

   If possible, get involved with the chamber of commerce as a resource. Also, many C of C offices will gladly and regularly give you lists of people who have made inquiries about housing in the area. Send them your business card, model home brochures, company information, a map of the area and other pertinent material. Include a concise, hand-written note letting them know how happy you and your company are about the possibility of serving them with all their new home needs.

   People moving into your area are often making an upscale career move and are frequently in the process of selling their current home (and therefore will be more likely to afford a new purchase).

   Those who respond to your note tend to be highly motivated

buyers and usually have little time during a visit to the area to make a decision. That combination can add up to clean, quick and satisfying sales.

6. **Read area newspapers alertly.**
   Don't hesitate to write personal notes to people featured in the newspaper:
   - Position changes and career moves are often printed in the business section. New salary status may trigger a desire to improve housing.
   - Birth announcements may indicate a need for a family to upgrade housing.
   - Engagements and weddings almost always signal a need for new housing. No longer are engaged couples the just-out-of-school types who must settle for a small apartment. Many of today's prospective brides and bridegrooms are upscale professionals who have a sizeable savings account and a need to project a higher status. Others are divorced or single parents who will combine separate households into a new home.

One important item in relation to sending congratulatory notes: Don't sell anything. Include your business card and a brochure, but use the note exclusively for offering your congratulations and best wishes.

7. **Never miss a chance to speak or write to the public.**
   Your foremost job is to be a master communicator, not just a new home salesperson. What better way to perfect your skills and position yourself as an authority than by speaking or writing to audiences of all sizes?

8. **Always ask for referrals from past buyers and from people who have looked at your homes and didn't buy.**

9. **Cultivate Realtors.**

You can avail yourself to mega-dollars worth of exposure by tapping into clubs, schools, civic organizations, Realtor associations and workshops that are always looking for a fresh, interesting speaker.

Don't hesitate to take advantage of any opportunity to write articles or be interviewed by newspaper or magazine writers. Also, you can avail yourself to wide exposure by appearing on area TV and radio talkshows (not specifically as a real estate salesperson, but as an authority on certain aspects of the business).

If you are unsure or fearful of public appearances (Who isn't?), take speech and writing classes at a community college or university in your area. Join Toastmasters International or take a Dale Carnagie course.

Position yourself, not as a salesperson, but as a real estate expert. Focus on such general topics as investing in real estate, creative financing, how to buy a new home or tax advantages resulting from home ownership. People are always interested in hearing or reading about topics that directly affect their pocketbooks.

Again, don't sell anything except yourself. The sales will follow, often in direct proportion to your genuine willingness to serve and inform the general public.

Take nothing for granted. Do more checking, more prodding, more observing and you will end up with more prospects than you can handle. That's a problem you would like to have, right?

A FINAL NOTE

Closing sales is directly related to finding plenty of prospects. With these simple strategies, you can become a *"slight-edge"* expert at prospecting.

In Chapter Five, I will share how to understand the prospects and the mixed messages they tend to transmit.

1. To sell new homes, you must have plenty of prospects.
2. Even though your company is responsible for the "attraction package," to join the top 5% of new home salespeople, you must develop additional prospects.
3. You can cultivate a program for finding lots of attractive prospects — with a little extra effort and creativity.

Chapter Five

HOW TO READ YOUR PROSPECT LIKE A BOOK

"Nam et ipsa scientia potestas est."
("Knowledge itself is power.") —FRANCIS BACON
(1561-1626)
English Philosopher and Statesman

VERBAL AND NONVERBAL OBSTACLES

Your job, as a master communicator and professional new home salesperson, is to identify and meet the needs of your prospects. This two-pronged task tends to be more difficult for a new home representative than for most other types of salespeople.

Here's why: First, with rare exception, the people in your sales office don't need a new home. They already have a place to live. People come into a new home sales center with built-in barriers. Generally, even if a person is very serious about buying a new home from you, no matter what you say or ask, he or she will respond with this predictable phrase: "I'm just looking."

Compare, for example, if ABC Company wants a computer. A management decision will be made: "We want a computer with these specific features." Someone from ABC will call several computer companies for competitive bids, and when the computer salesperson comes to call, the people at ABC who will make the decision will sit down and listen to the presentation. ABC management already recognizes a need, and the salesperson merely seeks to meet that need.

Not so with new home sales. The prospect will tell you, "I'm just looking" because they don't want to expose their need to the salesperson. It makes the process more difficult.

People aren't sales resistant; they are salespeople resistant.

First impressions aside, you have mere seconds to make contact with the prospect who has walked into your model home. In short order, you must determine the prospect's qualification by using the C.O.M.M.A. strategy:

C*ommitment* ("Are you serious?")
O*pportunity* ("What do you want/need?")
M*oney* ("Do you have the money?")
M*otivation* ("Why are you here?")
A*ction* ("When will you act?")

You may have only a minute or so to qualify that prospect (which I will amplify in SECTION III). You may have only a few more minutes to make your "Main Event" presentation (Chapter Nine). Obviously, you have to use all of your senses during those scant moments to decipher everything you can about the prospect.

There are as many reasons for a person not to buy a new home as there are to buy one. Here are reasons given, most often, as to why people look for a new home:

1. Financial opportunity
2. Status or ego
3. Location change
4. More space
5. Less space
6. Lifestyle change

However, there are reasons, either conscious or sub-conscious why they feel that they shouldn't. The fear of:

1. Financial obligation
2. Dealing with a builder
3. The mortgage application process
4. Change itself
5. The actual move
6. Making a commitment to all of the above

THE MESSAGE AND META-MESSAGE

As a professional communicator, you must constantly seek to understand what your prospect is thinking.

Dr. S. I. Hayakawa, well-known college president and former United States'senator from California, is known as the "Father of Semantics." Semantics is the study of words and word usage. Dr. Hayakawa was one of the first to contend that people say things all the time by using words, but they really don't always mean what they say.

For example, how often do people greet you by saying, "How are you doing today?" Do they really mean that, or are they just saying words to fill in what would otherwise be an awkward silence?

Test it out. The next time someone asks that question, answer, "I'm so glad you asked. I've been wanting to tell someone how I am doing and about all my problems. Do you have 15 minutes?"

Instantly, that person will tell you the truth, either with his eyes, mannerisms or spoken words.

All most friendly people really want to say is "Hello" or "Good morning." They don't really want to know how you are doing or feeling.

According to Dr. Hayakawa, what people say is the "message." What people really mean is the "meta-message." *Meta* is the Greek word for truth.

Prospects dish out the "message" to new home salespeople all the time.

They say:

"I've just started looking."

"I just want a brochure."

"I've only got a minute — I'm heading to the airport (or the mall, a funeral or . . .)

"The rooms are too small."

"Before I make any decisions, I have to talk to my friend in Atlanta."

Prospects give new home salespeople lots of statements, but what they are saying is not exactly what they mean. It is up to you to uncover the meta-message.

Remember, the fourth mindset of a *"slight-edge"* new home sales professional is to always seek and find the truth. Expending the extra effort to discover the difference between a prospect's message and meta-message will net mega-bucks in your bank account.

COMMUNICATION BARRIERS

Any new home salesperson, anyone who has ever tried unsuccessfully to convey benefits of a product to a prospect, knows how frustrating sales efforts can be.

The most common negative factor when a customer enters your sales office is fear. The prospect may not be aware of it, but 99% of lookers have a secret fear: running into YOU — the dreaded salesperson — and having to listen to your intensive, intrusive presentation. In a strange way, you represent the person who is going to reveal their need to spend money, pack, move and find new neighbors. That can be frightening to anyone.

Rather than admit their apprehension (to themselves and certainly not to you), they raise smokescreens and lift barriers.

The list of obstacles that can interfere with the transfer of sales information from one person to another runs the gamut from poor communication skills to preoccupation (on the part of the salesperson or the prospect).

Because communication is such a vital part of the sales process, it helps to know what blocks good communication and then try to go around (or over) those barriers. Lack of good communication, misunderstandings and mistakes are costly in lost sales and can result in problems with customers after the sale.

Here are 10 obstacles to communications which can occur during your sales presentation. If you recognize their existence, you have taken an important step toward overcoming them:

1. **Resistance to change.**

   People, including prospects who have voluntarily visited your model home, are reluctant to change anything they are comfortable with to try something new.

Habit is difficult to overcome. Buying a new home, however desirable, takes effort and is a journey into the unknown. You have to show the prospect that the benefits and advantages far outweigh any perceived problems.

2. **Lack of interest.**

Unless you have evidence to the contrary (through qualifying/questioning), you don't know that the prospect really is "just looking."

3. **Distractions.**

During a presentation, many things happen over which you have little control. Ringing telephones, other salespeople and their customers, noise and weather — these are a few of the obstacles you have to overcome to make sure that your prospect understands what you are saying.

4. **Lack of knowledge.**

No matter how well you understand what you are saying, the prospect may not. Avoid sales and real estate jargon, and use lots of questions to make sure your prospect comprehends everything that you present.

5. **Poor memory.**

You deal everyday with a wide range of intellects and emotional packages. Even if the prospect understands you, he or she will only retain 15%-20%, that's less than one fact out of every five. You must go to great lengths to involve the potential customer (cause them to experience it) in the information you are presenting using tie-downs and other involvement strategies (Chapter Eleven).

6. **Personal problems.**

You have no idea what is bouncing around in your prospect's mind during the presentation. You, the salesperson, may remind him or her of a hated lover or a cherished friend. Things you say or do may cause a mind-drift toward personal problems.

You cannot solve emotional problems, but you must keep the person with you — mentally — if you want to close him or her. Ask questions, lots of questions!

7. **Distorted thinking.**

We all tend to think what we want to, which sometimes distorts what we think we hear. Clarify everything to make sure you and the prospect are both hearing and understanding the same thing, or the distorted perceptions will come back to haunt you.

8. **False assumptions.**
   The salesperson may assume that the prospect understands or accepts certain statements when the exact opposite may be true.

How do you know what the prospect is thinking unless you probe carefully? Never assume *anything* but the sale!

9. **Emotional blocks.**
   When emotions — good or bad — are aroused, they can block out listening and can give wrong interpretations to what is said by either party.

10. **Language/cultural barriers.**
   We live in a diverse society, and many of your prospects may come from other regions or countries.
   No one wants to appear ignorant or uninformed. When you talk too fast, use local slang or make complicated statements, the prospect may nod agreeably and never ask for an explanation.
   It is up to you to simplify everything you say, especially when language or cultural barriers are present.
   When you understand the barriers to communication, you can plan and prepare your sales presentation to avoid as many of them as possible. Employ the K.I.S.S. principle. Keep it short and simple.

GET YOUR PROSPECT TO RELAX

One of the best ways to put your prospect at ease is to send very non-threatening messages.

Don't say "relax." Insensitivity and boorishness will only build larger barriers. Instead, use your own relaxed body expressions to help your prospect relax.

Here are 10 of the best nonverbal, relaxing messages you can send as a new home sales professional:

1. **Slow down your own body movements.**
   People expect salespeople to be quick and mechanical. Surprise them. Let your enthusiasm come out in your presentation, not your body movements.

2. **Assume a comfortable posture.**
   Be relaxed and open, not looking as if you were about to pounce on your victim.

3. **Develop increased eye contact.**
   Strive to appear natural with your eye contact, not overbearing or threatening.

4. **Smile frequently, not just with your mouth, but by smiling with your eyes.**

   Try it, it works! (As my friend, colleague and well known new homes sales trainer, Charlie Clark says, "Too many salespeople look like they have been weaned on a pickle."

5. **Don't overdo your facial expressions, and nod very slowly as you listen.**
   Fast movements and overdone expressions tend to appear gimmicky.

6. **Let your shoulders relax.**
   Raised, military-like shoulders indicate anxiety.

7. **Avoid gestures that communicate tension.**
   Nonverbal signals may include your hand on your face, hands clasped into a fist, arms akimbo or fast movements. Tense gestures may cause your prospect to suspect something amiss — "I wonder what this salesperson is so uptight about?"

8. **Be conscious about slightly slowing down your rate of speech.**
   Never match your prospect's higher rate of speech. Let your excitement about the new home come out in ways other than a verbal machine-gun.

9. **Stop talking at once when your prospect interrupts.**
   You want him or her to talk. As long as you know what you want to cover in your presentation, you should have no fear about getting derailed.
   Give your prospect the floor anytime he or she wants it. Nod your head slowly, no matter what they say.

10. **When you ask questions, combine your inquiry with your head slightly tilted to the side.**
    This unspoken message lets the prospect know that you are sincerely interested.

Remember, a relaxed prospect is more open to new ideas and information. Why struggle to pierce barriers when you can get people to relax *and* take them down?

DISCERN YOUR PROSPECT'S BODY LANGUAGE

Interpreting the feelings and reactions of your prospects is one of the most vital components of your sales ability. In fact, as you seek to uncover the meta-message, people will often express more by what they DO than by what they SAY.

Here are six of the 600 or so ways you can use nonverbal language to discover what is going on:

1. **Power hints.**
   Confidence, superiority and a dominant attitude are *suggested* by fingertip touching, hands behind the head, piercing eye contact and standing while others sit.

2. **Insecurity hints.**
   Handwringing, fidgeting, bowed head, minimal eye contact, throat clearing and twitching are *possible* indications that a person is submissive, nervous and insecure.

3. **Disagreement hints.**
   Skepticism, disagreement and even anger are *sometimes* evidenced when a person's body is angled extremely toward or away from you, when the face is tense, or when the arms are crossed.

4. **Boredom hints.**
   Ceiling watching, fiddling, shuffling papers, picking at clothing, foot tapping, a blank stare or looking out the window — all are *potential* indications of disinterest.

5. **Evaluation hints.**
   Glasses in mouth, hand on chin, nodding, index finger to mouth and good eye contact *can be* thought cues.

6. **Indecision hints.**
   Uncertainty *may be* shown by a pencil in mouth, head scratching, head down or cleaning of glasses.

However, **be careful!** Body language is ***not*** an exact science. The prospect could be sending signals that are completely unrelated to your presentation. What any signal means to the salesperson is that the person is thinking *something*. It is the professional's obligation, upon perceiving body signals, to ask questions which will clarify the situation.

This is important to understand. Do not be misled into assuming that specific body language signals definitely mean a certain emotion. As Charles Clarke, III, another friend, colleague and top notch consultant and trainer teaches in his program "Bulls, Owls, Lambs and Tigers", it depends. Depends on who they are and what their comfort zone is. The *"slight-edge"* veteran constantly looks for body language signals, if for no other reason than to provide another opportunity to ask questions and get inside the customer's thought process.

When you see body language signals, ask these types of questions: "How does this look to you?" or "what are your thoughts on this?"

Learn to assess a person's attitude by combining both verbal and body language cues. Total feedback is the key to reading a person.

A FINAL NOTE

Be careful. Don't assume anything without scanning the combination of a person's verbal AND body signals. What you see is not always what you get, as any poker player, news reporter or salesperson can tell you!

When you do develop a proficiency at reading people, be careful what you do with that information.

Says Mark McCormack, the best-selling author of *What They Don't Teach You at Harvard Business School,* of information gleaned from nonverbal signals:

> "The idea of using what you have learned properly is not to tell them how insecure you think they are or to point out all the things you have perceptively intuited that they may be doing wrong. If you let them know what you know, you will blow any chance of using your own insight effectively."

In chapters Six, Seven and Eight, you will learn to use that information discreetly and effectively.

1. Your job, as a master communicator and professional new home salesperson, is to identify and meet the needs of your prospects.

2. Your initial tasks are to get past the prospect's barriers to discover his or her meta-message.

3. You can make great strides toward understanding your prospect's meta-message by using nonverbal signals to get him or her to relax, and then to discern the customer's body language.

Chapter Six

DON'T SELL NEW HOMES. . .
TUNE IN TO RECEIVE WII-FM? SIGNALS

"Life is a romantic business. It is painting a picture, not doing a sum; but you have to make the romance, and it will finally come to the question of how much fire you have in your belly."

—OLIVER WENDELL HOLMES
(1809-1894) American Writer and Physician

NEW HOME SALES FACTS OF LIFE

The sooner you understand the selling process — in the most elementary sense — the better you will be prepared to face every prospect with confidence and enthusiasm.

"Slight-edge" new home sales veterans have learned these four basic sales realities:

1. **A customer will only pay attention to a person whom he or she believes has something important to say.**

   According to communications experts, the typical person must filter through 1,800 action messages every day. As a new home representative, your presentation must be very good merely to get past their "filtering system." To close a high percentage of customers, your presentation must be *extraordinary!*

2. **A customer will only buy for his or her own reasons, not for the salesperson's sake.**

   Champion salespeople know that every customer has an inner radio which is pre-tuned to pick up only one station — WII-FM? (What's In It For Me?).

   Failing to understand or act on this fact is the greatest single selling mistake a salesperson can make. Unless you use questions and tie-downs to discover what is "playing" on the prospect's WII-FM?, you might as well be doing your presentation with marbles in your mouth.

3. **A customer wants to BUY; he or she does not want to be SOLD**.

   Customers want to make up their own minds about the things they do and buy. They resent feeling coerced, manipulated or tricked.

4. **Buying is basically an emotional response.**

   The decision to buy may be tempered by logic, guided by common sense or delayed by conflicting interests, but what eventually causes the customer to own it is, to some degree, emotion.

In a sentence coined by Zig Ziglar, this is the great *"slight-edge"* secret which top-paid new home sales veterans have discovered:

"Show your prospect what he or she most desires, and that person will move heaven and earth to get it!"

A PROSPECT'S QUESTIONS

First and foremost, you are a professional communicator. You are not primarily a new home salesperson. Nowhere is that fact more certain than in the area of dealing with a prospect's WII-FM?

Before any new home salesperson can close a sale, the prospect has to say yes to all these seven questions:

1. **Can I RELATE to and TRUST the salesperson?**
   Establish rapport quickly (more about that in Chapter Seven and SECTION III).

2. **Will I UNDERSTAND what the salesperson says?**
   Get attention, ask questions, isolate the need quickly?

3. **Do I NEED the benefits proposed?**
   Establish the need through questions and keen awareness. Make sure the prospect understands his or her need and the benefits of having it satisfied with a new home.

4. **Does the product GIVE these benefits?**
   Appeal to the prospect's buying motives. Pick the features and benefits which will lead to conviction that your product best satisfies the need.

5. **Is this the best SOURCE for the product?**
   "Should-I-keep-shopping-around?" wonders the prospect. You must answer that question completely. Position yourself, your company and your product in the best possible light.

6. **Is the PRICE reasonable?**
   Convince the prospect that your value is high and your price is fair for all the many benefits obtained. This does not necessarily mean that it is the lowest price obtainable. Repeat the features, advantages and benefits to show that the investment is worth the pleasure of satisfying the need.

7. **Should I BUY?**
   This is usually the final decision in the sale. The salesperson must emphasize the advantages and pleasures which start with the purchase of a new home and the disadvantages of delay and missed enjoyment.

A component of this question is "WHEN should I buy?" You must convince the prospect that he or she should buy NOW to start enjoying the benefits of new home ownership immediately.

Understand the need for the prospect to find answers to these seven questions before buying, then help him or her get to "yes" for ALL of the inquiries.

WHY DO CUSTOMERS BUY?

Just as the prospect has seven basic questions that you must answer, he or she also will only buy for one or more of these three basic reasons:

1. **Fear** — safety, protection, future security, protection of investment.

2. **Need** — comfort, housing, pride, to save money, quality, style, desire for approval, social acceptance.

3. **Greed** — desire for gain, desire to possess, advancement, prestige and social status, luxury.

You will never be a highly paid new home sales professional until you understand and tap into one or more of these motives as you deal with each prospect.

UNDERSTANDING YOUR FEATURES AND BENEFITS

How do you uncover the secret desires of your prospect? You do it with lots of questions and a dynamic presentation. Moreover, you cannot power-pack your presentation until you maximize your features and benefits.

Unfortunately, most new home salespeople do not understand the difference between these two words.

If you are going to tie everything together that I have shared in this chapter — the painful realities of selling, a prospect's questions and the reasons why buyers buy — you must be able to explain the differences between your homes' features and benefits.

Features are the actual characteristics of a product or service. Features support the value of your benefits. Your features include your builder/company, location, amenities and the actual home themselves. Features *tell* who you are and what you have to offer.

Benefits are often expressed in terms of dollars saved or enhanced, time saved or maximized and/or reduction of risk. It's just that simple and never any more complicated. Benefits *sell* the prospect on fear, need or greed.

Do people buy houses or floorplans or gold faucets? No! People buy style, comfort, pleasure, happiness, security, enrichment opportunities, cinnamon-y kitchen smells, home life, self-respect and admiration.

Features tell. **Benefits** sell. In SECTION III, you will see how absolutely vital this one fact can be in your "Main Event" presentation.

If you are receiving a lot of price objections as you give your current presentation, you are probably doing a less-than-adequate job of creating a perception of value through your features and benefits. If the benefit can be made precisely clear, and if you can get the person to "buy in" to enough benefits, selling becomes much easier.

A FINAL NOTE

People don't want to buy things; they want to invest in their future. Once a prospect steps into your model home, your over-riding motivation must be to de-code the person's WII-FM? After you determine that meta-message, you can tailor your information to meet the prospect's specific needs and wants. That is one of the most powerful secrets of new home selling!

In Chapter Seven, you will learn how to discover everything you need to know about your prospects by becoming a question-master.

1. A prospect will only pay attention to people whom he or she believes has something important to say.
2. A prospect only buys for his or her WII-FM? reasons, not for the salesperson's motives.
3. A prospect wants to BUY; he or she does not want to be SOLD.
4. Buying is very often an emotional response.
5. Any customer buys for one of these three basic reasons: fear, need or greed.
6. Features *tell*. Benefits *sell*.

Chapter Seven

QUESTION YOUR WAY TO NEW HOME SALES SUCCESS-*Colombo Lives!*

"The interviewer must be curious about everything."

—LARRY KING Talkshow Host

IS THIS SELLING?

Imagine how life would be if doctors acted as many salespeople do. You might walk into a doctor's office one day and be greeted with a scenario like this:

"I fell and hurt my left arm," you begin. "I don't think it's broken, but it might be sprained or something."

"Your arm? Boy, are you in luck today!" the salesperson/doctor says, smiling broadly.

"I don't feel so lucky," you respond. It hurts like crazy!"

"D'you know why this is your lucky day?" the physician asks hungrily, totally ignoring your comment. "We're running an incredible close-out sale on artificial limbs . . .we're getting ready for the new models!"

"Doc'" you protest, "My arm hurts, but I don't need an artificial limb, for cryin' outloud!"

"What better time than now?" he continues talking smoothly, "I can fix you up with this `Arnold Schwartzenagger' model! It's just like the one the big guy used in his latest movie — *Terminator* — the flick where he plays yet another alien robot. This baby is loaded with options, and you can get it, today only, for the unbelievably low price of $100,000! That's a savings of nearly $25,000. Don't you agree that this is an incredible deal?"

The doctor nods gently until you acknowledge positively, then he adds, "Besides, it's all covered by your insurance. Look at the muscles ripple on that baby! Could I schedule you for installation Tuesday, or would Thursday be more convenient for you?"

You would RUN — not walk — to the nearest exit!

BECOME A "COLOMBO"

The story about the doctor and his "Arnold Schwartzanegger" artificial arm is fictitious, or is it? Salespeople who subscribe to this "jawbone theory" (some call it the "shotgun theory") of selling often lose sales because they focus more on *what the salesperson wants to happen* than on *what the prospect wants to happen.*

You can overcome this lethal weakness by learning to question and listen well. You must look beneath the surface to discover and reveal what is going on in the prospect's mind and heart. You must become COLOMBO!

He is one of television's perennial favorites, that detective in the rumpled raincoat, with his beat-up car and gravelly voice.

The premise in every Colombo program is basically the same: by the first commercial break, the audience and Colombo both know who committed the crime. Right?

If Peter Falk's character were like other gumshoes, such as Sergeant Friday or Dirty Harry, he would escort the criminal into a dimly-lit, poorly ventilated room, shine a blinding light into the dastardly person's face, and use high-pressure tactics to force a confession. (That would be pushy!)

Not Colombo! He is a master communicator. He uses cunningly-designed wiles to get people to trust him and open up to him. What style!

Throughout each program he remains non-threatening. He keeps asking questions. If he doesn't get enough information with one question, he rephrases the same inquiry:

"I'm just curious. . ."
"Could you help me out with this?"
"Just one more thing. . ."
"Can we go over this again so I can understand?"

Questions! You need to become a master at asking questions.

Curiosity may have killed the cat, but it is the *pro* in professional selling.

QUESTION YOUR WAY TO SUCCESS

The single-most valuable tool of the new home sales professional is the skillfully asked question. In fact, the best way to tell a mediocre salesperson from the well-paid veteran is to listen to that person's questions during the presentation.

Questions enable you to do three very important things:

1. **Questions permit you to discover what the prospect wants and the conditions upon which he or she will buy what you're selling.**
   I have already mentioned C.O.M.M.A. qualifying, and will explain this topic more completely during the "Main Event."

2. **Questions make the prospect feel important, and allow him or her to identify, clarify and express their wants or needs.**
   By skillfully and sensitively probing, you can take the guesswork out of selling — and buying.

3. **Questions involve the prospect in the selling process.**
   Involvement is crucial. Questions help discover and correct misconceptions that could derail a sale.

Avoid the amateurish technique of holding up one floorplan after another and asking "Is this it?" Become a highly respected professional who renders a valuable service, a service for which you can expect to be paid very well.

TYPES OF QUESTIONS

Behind every question you ask should be a basic reason for asking it. By making your reason clear in the framing of a question, you are much more apt to get the desired response.

A **FACTUAL QUESTION** seeks to get information. Position your question by beginning with What? When? Where? Why? Who? and How?

The **ALTERNATIVE CHOICE QUESTION** tries to get agreement or a decision: "Which of these floorplans do you like best" or "do you prefer oak or walnut?"

The **EXPLANATORY QUESTION** helps you obtain additional information or to broaden the discussion: "How would this help you?"

A **JUSTIFYING QUESTION** gets proof. It can also help you challenge the prospect's old ideas and to come up with new solutions: "I'm just curious why you said that?"

A **LEADING QUESTION** introduces one of your ideas: "What do you think of this. . . ?"

HYPOTHETICAL QUESTIONS use assumptions and "trial balloons: "What would happen if we did it this way?"

COORDINATIVE QUESTIONS develop a common agreement and point toward taking action: "Do we all agree that this is our next step?"

If you can realize the value of becoming a master at the art of asking questions, your presentations-to-closings ratio will dramatically change! People love to hear themselves talk. If you provide them with that opportunity by asking questions, sales will automatically follow.

HOW TO ASK THE RIGHT QUESTIONS

Here are 10 principles for becoming a new home sales Colombo:

1. **Prepare, in advance, the questions you will ask.**
   There is one caution: be careful not to phrase them so they sound canned.

2. **Ask open-ended and indirect questions.**
   Closed questions that call for a "yes" or "no" answer tend to discourage people from talking, to give only limited information, and to set a negative tone. Open-ended questions help prospects tell you how they feel, what they want, or what they think.

3. **Ask need-development questions.**
   You want to do more than get the prospect to talk — you want that prospect to tell you what he or she needs. Frame questions which will give you insight into the way the prospect perceives his or her needs.

4. **Ask questions which help you identify dominant needs.**
   Usually one overriding need rises in the prospect's mind — a need you can pinpoint by asking the right questions.

5. **Ask questions which help you focus on the dominant buying motivations — WII-FM?**
   Buying motivations and needs are not always the same. The reasons center on desires, feelings and personal tastes.

6. **Avoid offensive questions or asking questions in an insensitive way.**
   Some examples of pitfalls to avoid are "set-up," nosey or intimidating inquiries. Do not condescend.

7. **Start with broad queries, then move toward more narrow questions.**
   Broad inquiries are usually less threatening and produce more general information. They can help you get things rolling and steer you in the right direction. However, as your probing becomes more comfortable and picks up speed, you will need to get more specific with your questions.

8. **Ask questions that are easy to answer.**
   Questions that require technical or specific knowledge can make the prospect feel stupid. The more savvy you make your prospect feel, the better he or she will respond to you.

9. **Use questions to guide the interview and keep it positive in tone.**
   Some prospects love to ramble, but by skillfully using questions you can keep the interview focused and moving in the right direction.
   Ask questions that people can easily respond to in a positive manner. Studies have shown that most people much prefer to agree than to assert themselves and disagree. Make it easy to react positively.
   One note: avoid explosive subjects such as religion, politics, race and deep personal problems.

10. **Ask — then be quiet and listen.**
   The prospect cannot give you information as long as you keep talking.
   People who talk themselves out of sales do at least 80% of the talking and only 20% of the listening. But new home sales professionals do 80% of the listening and 20% of the talking.

The difference can be astounding in terms of your presentations-to-closings percentages!

Questions are your greatest selling tool. The better you become at asking questions, the easier it will be for you to sell. M. R. Kopmeyer, the well-known speaker and author, says: "People who *demand* anything, anytime, are confrontational. That closes people up. Those, however, who *suggest* often get anything they want."

L.I.S.T.E.N. PROSPECTS INTO BUYING

Asking questions is vital. We have established that fact. But listening to the answers to those questions is even more important.

For years, the selling climate was geared toward satisfying the needs and interests of the salesperson! But that has changed. Your objective is to focus on the prospect's needs. To meet that objective, you must L.I.S.T.E.N. your prospect into buying:

L*ook* at the person with whom you are talking.
Be aware of his or her facial expressions and body language.

I*nvolve* yourself in the conversation by saying:
"That's interesting."
"I know what you mean."
"Then what happened?"

S*teady* yourself, no matter what the prospect says or does.
If you maintain calm and keep listening, you can provide stabilization.

T*ranslate* the meaning of your prospect's remarks. Read between the lines so you can better understand what his or her needs are.

E*xcursions* are taboo. Tune-in to the speaker. Boring people are easily distracted. Never interrupt the prospect.

N*eeds* are paramount. Be concerned with the buyer's desires, and balance those needs with your personal and corporate interests.

Your objective is to L.I.S.T.E.N. each prospect into buying, not to "get in your two cents worth." If all you want to talk about is yourself — your interests, your products, your product's features, your company — you will undoubtedly encounter strong sales resistance.

But if you focus your attention upon the prospect's interests, needs, desires and values, you will notice a remarkable difference in that person's openness to you.

A FINAL NOTE

The better you become at asking questions and actively listening, the more often you can accomplish mutually-satisfying objectives. This "Colombo" approach to probing separates the well-paid professionals from impoverished amateurs.

Remember Zig Ziglar's classic statement: "You can get everything you want out of life if you help enough other people get what they want."

In SECTION III, you will learn how to turn what you learn from your questions into an understanding about the prospect and create productive, powerful presentations!

A COMMUNICATIONS QUIZ

How well do you take charge of the sales atmosphere? How well do you control the space and time you work in?

Rate yourself on how well you control the sales atmosphere:

5 — "I do that all the time?"
4 — "That's me, most of the time?"
3 — "I'm like that half of the time?"
2 — "I'm not like that too much?"
1 — "That's not me at all!"

When I speak with others in a sales climate, I am always in control of:

____ (1) Time (how fast or slow I talk, my pauses).
____ (2) Space (how I move, bodily, and where I move to).
____ (3) Voice (volume, pitch and tone, pronunciation).
____ (4) Questions (variety, open-ended, informational).
____ (5) Eye contact (messages sent and received).
____ (6) My attitude (how I feel — open, friendly, warm).
____ (7) My state of mind (confident, calm, enthusiastic).
____ (8) My feelings (I know what they are and am clear).
____ (9) The conversation flow (natural, genuine interest).
____ (10) The balance (give-and-take, I don't dominate).

SCORING:	50	Perfect!
	Over 40	Excellent sales atmosphere control
	35 to 39	Good
	25 to 34	Average
	Below 25	You desperately need to work on your communication skills.

1. Become a new home sales "Colombo!"

2. Question your way to success.

3. Become proficient at using FACTUAL, ALTERNATIVE CHOICE, EXPLANATORY, JUSTIFYING, LEADING, HYPOTHETICAL and COORDINATIVE questions.

4. L.I.S.T.E.N. prospects into buying.

Chapter Eight

BUILD A POWERFUL SELLING VOCABULARY

"When dealing with people, remember you are not dealing with creatures of logic, but with creatures of emotions -- creatures bristling with prejudice, and motivated by pride and vanity."

—DALE CARNEGIE

WORDS

Years ago, I learned from legendary sales trainer Tom Hopkins that the vocabulary we use in selling or trying to persuade others could cost us millions of dollars annually in lost sales. I have included a number of his suggested alternatives, such as "buy", "contract", "deal", "monthly payment", "pitch", and "sign", along with others I have developed.

Words to you, a professional communicator, are the tools of your trade. The size and power of your vocabulary influences your ability to persuade. Your ability to persuade either expands or limits your capacity to communicate with others.

Surprisingly, research points to the fact that vocabulary expansion usually stops when the average man or woman reaches 25 years of age.

Why? We get busy. We think we don't need to learn any more words. We don't realize that success increases in proportion to the strength of our vocabularies.

As a new home salesperson, you must be able to communicate effectively and powerfully. If your language has been reduced to jargon and buzz words, here are some techniques that can get you started toward a power vocabulary:

1. Keep a good dictionary and thesaurus at home and in the office --- and use them.

2. Read books, magazines and newspapers voraciously.

3. Look up unfamiliar words and memorize their meanings.

4. Make an effort to use words whose meanings you know but rarely bring into conversation.

5. Look up all the synonyms of words you use regularly and start using those synonyms in conversation.

6. Take a course or read a book on building vocabulary.

7. Read "It Pays to Enrich Your Word Power" every month in Reader's Digest, and use the words at least 10 times in your sentences.

Why bother?

In every area of your life, you are either going forward or backward. Even if you only integrate one-third of these new words in everyday language, the freshness and innovation you experience will translate into an intriguing enthusiasm.

Vocabulary is important. It is one of the great foundations to a natural, flowing presentation.

PROFESSIONAL PERSUADERS USE POWERFUL WORDS

Everything you say to a prospective buyer should lead naturally toward the closing. As you seek to become a master communicator, you must learn what words to use, when to use them, and how to use them most effectively.

Think about using words in your presentation which build emotion. Since much of buying is based on some level of emotion, you need to learn to build emotion with your words. Especially during your presentation, those emotion-filled words must be positive, not negative.

Think about this: your model center represents a new home "Disney World." People come there to get excited. You are Mickey Mouse and Captain EO in one person. You are going to take the prospect on a grand tour of "Fantasyland."

At the same time, people come to the new home model center with negative barriers. They obviously would like to own a new home, or they would not be curious. On the surface, prospects arrive with a desire to look at you, your company, your product and its amenities. Subconsciously, however, they are trying to find reasons not to make an investment decision. It's crazy, but that's the way it is!

Let's face it — the decision to purchase a new home is not easy. It marks a major commitment. It means moving, leaving loved ones and friends, going to different churches, enrolling in new schools, finding good orthodontists and establishing an entirely untested lifestyle.

When you face prospects who are mentally looking for reasons *not* to make the decision to purchase a new home, you must use words that build a positive emotion.

Negative words can breed negative thoughts. Those negative thoughts can breed negative actions. You must reverse that process.

For example, when you see or hear these words, TERRIBLE or AWFUL, what do you think?

They create a negative or an adverse feeling. Yet how many times have you heard a co-worker (or yourself) say, "I have an awfully nice house I'd like to show you." Or, "Isn't that a terribly pleasant location?"

When you think about them, awfully and nice don't fit together. Neither do terribly and pleasant. Such combinations create a conflict between the prospect's conscious awareness and the subconscious understanding, which are already in turmoil because of the like-to-buy/don't-want-to-buy clash.

There is a better way!

POWER WORDS AND PHRASES FOR NEW HOME SELLING

Create a vocabulary of positive, powerful words that will foster affirmative images in the prospect's conscious and subconscious minds.

Likewise, eliminate all of the words used frequently by new home salespeople which would create negative images and have a detrimental impact on your presentation.

Let me go through my all-time, need-to-change list of words and phrases (I've put them in alphabetical order for your convenience and future reference):

DON'T SAY	INSTEAD SAY
AGENT When people hear this term, they think of FBI, IRS and Soviet. "Agent" seems too sinister and gives people the opportunity to think negative thoughts.	**REPRESENTATIVE** "Yes, Ms. Jones, I am the representative with whom you spoke over the telephone."
"BE-BACK" Never use industry or office slang-words. We know what they mean, but the customer doesn't.	**CUSTOMER OR PROSPECT** This is what they are! They are living, breathing, potential home-owners, not impersonal, jargon-ish statistics.
BUY People don't like to buy things because it means giving up money.	**OWN, GET INVOLVED or ACQUIRE** If you can get them to own it, they will buy it!
CHEAPER "Cheap" degrades value.	**LESS EXPENSIVE OR MORE AFFORDABLE** "Yes, Mr. Jones, it is less expensive than . . ."
COMMISSION This word sounds as if you are taking money directly out of the customer's pocket.	**PROFESSIONAL SERVICE FEE** This phrase heightens value and de-emphasizes cost.

DON'T SAY	INSTEAD SAY
COMPLEX This sounds confusing and institutional.	**FACILITIES or AMENITIES** "Mr. Jones, let me show you our exciting recreational facilities."
CONDOMINIUM "Condominium" is actually a Latin word which defines a specific type of real estate ownership. It does not clarify a style of residence or dwelling. This term often conjures up negative emotions connected with apartments, association meetings or "rules".	**HOME OR RESIDENCE** Everyone wants to live in a home!
CONTRACT "Contract" has an immediate, red-flag, negative connotation of lawyers, binding clauses, trouble and "How do I get out of it?"	**AGREEMENT OR PAPERWORK** "Mr. and Mrs. Jones, I'll get the paperwork started," or "Ms. Smith, take a moment to look at the agreement while I get those carpet samples."
COST The *cost* is always too much.	**TOTAL VALUE** Talk value, not price. People want to invest, not spend money. "The total value of this home is $ ____________".
DEAL Face it, most of the time when you "get a deal" or "make a deal," someone winds up getting the proverbial "short-end of the stick." We live in a world of "bad deals," "a deal that is too good to believe" and "drug deals." Eliminate this word completely from your vocabulary.	**GREAT OPPORTUNITY or TRANSACTION** Everyone wants to take advantage of a "great opportunity," and most don't mind making a "transaction" if benefits are emphasized.

DON'T SAY	INSTEAD SAY
DOWN PAYMENT The "down payment" implies future payments.	**INITIAL DEPOSIT or INITIAL EQUITY** An "initial equity" points positively toward the future.
ELEVATION This can be confusing, especially since "elevation" means the height above sea level to many people.	**THE ARCHITECTURAL STYLE or EXTERIOR APPEARANCE**
EXECUTE Gas chambers and firing squads — scary!	**APPROVE, O.K. AUTHORIZE OR ENDORSE** "Mr. Jones, would you please approve this paperwork."
HOUSE This is a cold, factual term. It speaks of blueprints, wood and nails. Nobody wants to live in a lifeless structure.	**HOME OR RESIDENCE** Connotation: Thanksgiving dinners, Christmas mornings, warmth, a safe haven and freshly-baked cookies.
INVENTORY If the customer understands what you are saying, he or she may think you are dying to "make a deal" on the "hard-to-move" house.	**COMPLETED HOME** (or nearly completed home). This positive term positions you well and creates an urgency to close. "Ms. Jones, I have a completed home that may be perfect for you!"
LAST CHANCE See INVENTORY.	**REMAINING OPPORTUNITY** or **AVAILABLE**
LEFT See INVENTORY.	**AVAILABLE**

DON'T SAY	INSTEAD SAY
LOT or PARCEL A "lot" doesn't sound like a lot! A "lot" or "parcel" implies a tiny tract or a weeded plot.	**HOME-SITE** This eliminates confusion and reduces any prejudgement towards the site.
MONTHLY DUES, FEES or ASSESSMENTS Connotation: closely akin to taxes.	**MONTHLY MAINTENANCE INVESTMENT OR CONTRIBUTION** Reasoning: an investment toward maintenance of their new property.
MONTHLY PAYMENT This implies a drudgery of writing checks and stretching the budget.	**MONTHLY INVESTMENT** This conveys value and a wise concern for the future.
OFFER This suggests a trading, "wheeler-dealer" mentality, a cost flexibility and a chance to make a lower "offer." As a new home salesperson, you must never say "Lets write up the offer."	**AGREEMENT or PAPERWORK** "Ms. Jones, do you have any questions about this paperwork?"
OPTIONAL, PREMIUMS or EXTRA CHARGES Examples: fireplace, custom cabinets or extras.	**ADDITIONAL INVESTMENT** "Mr. and Mrs. Jones, the additional investment for this custom-crafted fireplace will be $3000."
PITCH Sleazy amateurs make a "pitch."	**PRESENTATION** Well-paid professionals offer a planned, thorough "presentation."

DON'T SAY	INSTEAD SAY
PRICE No matter what it is, the *price* is always too much. Mentioning "price" invites an offer, because people always want the price to be less.	**TOTAL VALUE or INVESTMENT** People don't want to diminish their investment or lower the value of their investment.
PROJECT, SUB-DIVISION, DEVELOPMENT OR TRACT All four terms have negative connotations. They imply trucks moving dirt, plumbers, carpenters and torn up streets.	**NEIGHBORHOOD, VILLAGE or COMMUNITY** If you are talking about a specific area, or "village" say "neighborhood." If you are describing a more general area, use "community." Both convey positive images of friendly neighbors, playing children and a healthy place to live.
PUD I keep hearing salespeople say, "We have a large PUD," or "We've been working on this PUD for a long time." Who cares? Don't ever use industry jargon, especially around customers. You don't impress when you are seeking to look important at their expense.	**PLANNED COMMUNITY** "Mr. and Mrs. Jones, we have one of the most exciting planned communities you will see!"
SELL People feel like they have already been sold too much.	**HELP YOU TO...** Help people to own, to acquire.

DON'T SAY	INSTEAD SAY
SIGN Since childhood we have all been indoctrinated: "Never sign anything until your father, mother, Aunt Bertha and a lawyer read it first!"	**APPROVE, O.K. AUTHORIZE or ENDORSE** Instead of asking the customers to "sign the contract," say, "Mr. and Mrs. Jones, would you okay the paperwork?" "Would you please approve this for me?" Or, "Would you authorize this change order?"
SPEC See PUD and INVENTORY. Don't use builder or sales slang.	**NEARLY COMPLETED HOME** "Mr. Jones, let me show you one of our nearly completed homes."
STANDARD Implies features that are common, ordinary, everyday and hardly exciting.	**INCLUDED FEATURES** Positions your features as valuable and necessary.
THE COMPANY, THEY "They have built this" sounds so impersonal. When you use "they" you disassociate yourself from the company and new homes that you are trying to sell.	**I, MINE, OUR, US or WE** Talk in terms of "my company" or "our company." Say, "Mr. and Mrs. Jones, we'll take care of that." Put everything in the first person — it builds credibility for your company and for you.
TRACT See PROJECT.	**PLANNED COMMUNITY**

DON'T SAY	INSTEAD SAY
UNIT What does this mean to the prospect? It may imply "small," "cramped" or run-of-the-mill. It elicits a negative emotional response. If the word was a positive emotional term, poets and songwriters might have given us such classics as "Unit Sweet Unit," "My Old Kentucky Unit" or "I'll be Unit for Christmas!"	**HOME OR RESIDENCE** These are warm, beautiful words.
"UP" See "BE-BACK." Even if your office operates on an "up" rotation basis, the customer should never hear a company employee say, "Mary, your UP is out here," or "Mary, you're UP."	**CUSTOMER OR PROSPECT** Treat them with warmth and as individuals. If you serve these wonderful people well, you maximize your opportunity to stay in business as a new home salesperson!

Oh, one more thing. When using the word "Realtor", make sure you pronounce it as a two syllable word, Real - tor, not Real-A-Tor. Just think of this. It's doc-tor, not doc-a-tor.

"But," you protest, "there are so many to learn. What a lot of work."

Right! But you don't have to learn them all today. Add to your vocabulary as many as you can each week. Tape them on a cassette, and listen to the list on your way to your office each morning, or acquire *The Five Minute Professional* cassette learning system and use it. Repetition works wonders.

Let me give you an example of the way you already use repetition to learn information. Take this quick quiz by mentally completing these three blanks:

"________________ tastes good like a ___________ should."

"I'd walk a mile for a ___________."

"______ is it!"

"I said I wanted a ____ Light!"

If you answered "Winston," "cigarette," "Camel," "Coke" and "Bud," you are absolutely correct.

Getting the final two answers correct is understandable, since the two companies which make those products are big spenders in the $15 billion-a-year advertising business.

But if you answered the first three blanks correctly (and 98% of my seminar attendees do), especially if the jingle came to your mind, you are proving the power of repetition. Cigarette manufacturers have not been allowed to buy television or radio advertising time for a quarter-century!

Put the power of repetition to work for you, and begin by learning a profitable new sales vocabulary.

CANCEL-CANCEL

How do you eliminate the negative words? Ask your subconscious mind to help you. Get familiar with the positive words. Write them down. Say them outloud.

Then spend a few minutes closing your eyes and picturing a blank screen. Make the screen any color you prefer. Then visualize these two words, using any script, color or type you desire:

CANCEL-CANCEL

Picture those two words, then see the words flashing on and off.

Open your eyes and without moving your lips, have your mind say those two words:

CANCEL-CANCEL

Say the words outloud:

CANCEL-CANCEL

From this moment, every time you catch yourself accidently saying one of the negative words — "sell," "unit" or "development" — simply think "CANCEL-CANCEL," then replace the ill-used terms with "help you to" "home" or "neighborhood."

Let me suggest in haste that you shouldn't do this outloud or move your lips. The customer will know for certain that you are bonkers!

Another point: you and your co-workers can help each other with this. Never correct each other within earshot of a customer, but during sales meetings and education sessions, catch each other using negative terms and say, "CANCEL-CANCEL!" Make it a game. Everyone has too much to gain to ignore this vital vocabulary change.

SPECIAL OCCASIONS FOR USING NEGATIVE WORDS AND PHRASES

There is only one occasional moment when you should purposefully use negative words. Remember, I've quoted Zig Ziglar before: "You can get anything you want out of life, as long as you help other people get what they want." This is true. You can "help" your competition get what they want by using their words to compare between you and them.

You have beautiful home sites, but the competition has lots and houses for sale. You have wonderful homes, but they have specs and units. You have great opportunities, but they have deals.

Now, I don't believe in tearing the competition down, but if they want to use those terms, allow them to.

When Ms. Jones, the customer, says, "The sales agent over at XYZ development says that his price is cheaper than yours, and that his standard features are better than yours," agree!

You can add, "That's a nice little subdivision. In fact, the prices in their project *are* cheaper, and I understand they do have some good standard features in their units. But let me take a moment to share with you about the wonderful benefits of our neighborhood, and the features which are included in our custom-crafted homes. . . ."

A FINAL WORD

In planning your presentation, think not only about what you want to say, but how you want to say it. Your choice of words and phrases can help create a positive emotional response in the buyer's mind.

Be creative! When you describe homes and features, paint vivid word pictures that will expand the prospect's visual impressions.

Build the vocabulary of a master communicator! You need to have a vast showcase of the right words to use in your presentation. Knowing what words to use, when to use them and how to use them will give you a natural, non-threatening control of the sales situation. More sales will quickly follow.

In Chapter Nine, I will help you put together the basic components of your planned presentation.

1. Build a master communicator's vocabulary.
2. Persuaders must use positive words to overcome subconscious, negative barriers.
3. Learn the power words and phrases for new home selling.
4. Learn to eliminate negative words from your sales vocabulary by using the "CANCEL-CANCEL" technique.
5. Only use negative words on "special" occasions.

Chapter Nine

THE FIVE-MINUTE PROFESSIONAL

"The world stands aside to let anyone pass who knows where he is going."

—DAVID STARR JORDAN

YOU'VE GOT FIVE MINUTES. . .GO!

A famous playwright once said to an aspiring protege, "If you can't write the plot on the back of your business card, you don't have a good plot!"

For the new home salesperson, the playwright's point is this — *if you cannot condense your information to a few vital components and present it quickly, you are not ready to be a* ***"slight-edge"****, new home sales professional.*

Imagine this:

Mr. Jones walks into your model home center. He hands you his business card, shakes your hand, introduces himself and says, "I'm being transferred into this city by my company and I need a three-bedroom, two-bath home. I have a wife and two children back in Center City, and we are moving in two months. I can afford a home between $125,000 and $150,000."

"Now," he continues, "I am going to make a decision on a house today. I've looked at 10 advertisements for new home communities that seem to fit the bill, and you are one of the 10. I can only spend five minutes with a salesperson at each location. Are you ready?"

Mr. Jones then looks at his watch and says, "Go!"

What would you do? The typical salesperson's reaction would be disbelief:

"Is this a prank, or what?"

> "Oh, there is no way I could tell you about everything that we offer in 30 minutes, much less five. . .maybe you'd better come back when you have more time."
>
> "I can't tell you much in such a short time, but here's a brochure and my card. Look through the information, and if you are interested, give me a call."

I've seen salespeople actually start stammering and talking incoherently under those conditions.

I firmly believe that every new home salesperson should be able to make a qualified presentation of the facts concerning the *builder, location, specific amenities and specific product* — in five minutes or less!

To top that, the salesperson should be able to fill those five minutes in an organized and concise manner, stating appropriate features and benefits and asking a number of significant questions.

"Impossible!" you say. Tell that to the thousands of *"Five-Minute Professional"* seminar-goers and audio cassette system owners who have used my concepts to transform average livelihoods into exciting high paying careers.

Producing a top-rated performance in five minutes or less is simply a matter of organizing and scripting the information, rehearsing it until it is well learned, being so sure of your lines that you can ad-lib confidently, and then being able to perform under pressure.

Recognize that I'm not talking about five minutes to make a total presentation, to qualify and to handle 15 different objections. I am talking about a conditioning exercise to help you put all the information down which must be given in a presentation.

Everything you have read in this book to this chapter has pointed you in the direction of being able to make this happen with assurance and style. Everything you read from this moment will add to your "Main Event" mastery.

DON'T MISS HIDDEN OPPORTUNITIES

Your purpose is not always to make a presentation in five minutes or less. Sometimes you will have much longer, more "normal" allotments of time.

But it is a fact of life that people whisk in and say the classic lines that you and I have heard zillions of times:

> "I'm in a hurry. . .I just want a brochure."
>
> "I'm on my way to the airport. . .my flight leaves soon. . .can I quickly pick up some basic information about your homes?"
>
> "I've got a chicken in the oven, but I want your floorplans to look over."
>
> "Grandma is waiting out in the car, so I need to get your stuff and hit the road!"

Stop all of those people and ask, "About how much time do you have?" I always do this. Nearly 90% say something such as this: "Oh, about five minutes."

They never say, "two minutes" or "three minutes and nine seconds." Never! It's almost always five minutes or more. These "just lookers" and "just want a brochure" people represent a vast, untapped gold mine if you are willing to prepare yourself for the many "five minutes" that come along every week.

Remember that your builder or the marketing department of your company spends $500 or more to bring each prospect through your sales office door, even the "just lookers." You have to be ready, no matter what happens.

THE FIVE-MINUTE DRILL

Just as the professional football team has a two-minute drill — some call it a no-huddle, set-pattern or hurry-up offense — that they use in the final moments of a close game, you must have your own FIVE-MINUTE DRILL, which you can perform under the most extreme pressure.

It is very important to be "unconsciously competent," to be able to do your best regardless of the tensions. The FIVE-MINUTE DRILL allows you to do that!

You must know your presentation extremely well through PDR (Practice-Drill-Rehearse), and I will give you plenty of opportunities to PDR.

PRESENTATION GUIDELINES

In each segment of your presentation — You and Your Builder, Your Location, Your Amenities and Your Product — you need to do three things:

PREVIEW — You must introduce what you plan to tell the prospect.
PRESENT — Tell it.
RECAP — Restate what you just told them, through the use of tie-downs and involvement questions.

By offering the same information three times, the retention level goes up considerably.

Also, during the presentation, you should offer at least six tie-downs, or involvement questions. For example:

"Aren't you?"
"Wouldn't it?"
"Can't you?"
"Haven't you?"

The skillful and effective use of tie-downs is so important that I will invest most of Chapter Eleven on that crucial subject.

YOU AND YOUR COMPANY

Why sell yourself and your company at the beginning? Unless you get the prospect to trust you first, and trust the builder second, you might as well flush the remainder of the presentation.

Sell you and your company first. There are only three things you need to say about the builder:

Who are we?

Research your company for information. Are you large or small? Create a one- or two-sentence statement about your organization.

What have we done?

Again, research the history of your company and create a one- or two-sentence statement about those accomplishments. What have you achieved? Have you won awards from the city or from the National Association of Home Builders? How many homes have you built?

What does that mean to the prospect?

Remember the WII-FM? Build credibility and value. This is the first place in the outline where you use one of the six carefully constructed tie-down statements. You can recap and use this involvement question at the same time:

"Mr. and Mrs. Jones, I wanted to mention those important facts about my company. I would imagine today that — as with most other folks — the financial stability and the reputation for integrity and quality construction offered by the company that builds your new home is probably important to you, isn't it?"

As Mae West and Joe Namath used to say, "If you've got it, flaunt it!" Position yourself and your company as established professionals.

Don't forget to PREVIEW, PRESENT and RECAP.

YOUR LOCATION

"The three most important things about real estate are location, location and location." How many times have you heard that venerable adage? Like it or not, it is still true.

Location is probably the singular factor that separates one builder and community from another. Essentially, most companies can construct homes for approximately the same amount of money per square foot, provided quality is comparable. But the one thing that causes prices and values to fluctuate is the cost of land. That cost is a direct result of desirability of location.

Your location is far more important than your brochures or floorplans. If the prospect likes your location, there is a high probability that you have a floorplan to suit their needs.

Position your macro- and micro-locations well!

Your *macro-location* refers to the general area or where you are in relation to the rest of the world. This may include what side of town you are on and the transportation features (airports and highway access). Don't forget to mention the features and benefits of nearby shopping centers, lakes and recreation areas, coliseums, universities, restaurants and hospitals. These are the things that make your general area a great place in which to live.

Script five specific features and accompanying benefits of your macro-location. On one, use another tie-down question:

> "Mr. Jones, in the description of our general area, I've mentioned that we are only 22 minutes from our international airport. You mentioned that your job requires you to travel by plane a lot, and wouldn't it be convenient to be so close to a large airport ?

Next is the micro-location or neighborhood. Who are the people in your neighborhood? Again, script five key features and benefits — schools, churches, shopping, the quality of homes surrounding your community. The more you know personally about each feature, the more pizazz you can put into the benefits. Give an appropriate tie-down to one of the key points:

> "With Billy and Suzy both in elementary school this next year, wouldn't it be convenient for them to be able to walk just three blocks to XYZ School with the other children from our neighborhood? In fact, the new principal and her husband moved into one of our homes just last week."

YOUR AMENITIES

Amenities are anything that is outside the home or the specific homesite itself. In some planned communities, the amenities that you have to offer can be very elaborate, running the gamut from 18-hole championship golf courses to top-flight tennis facilities. You may have a unique entranceway to the community, 24-hour security or a posh swimming pool.

Amenities may also include such basics as underground utilities, beautiful sidewalks, streetlights and landscaping. Be creative!

Again, make a list of your neighborhood's five most important amenities, and script these with features and benefits. Create an appropriate tie-down for each:

> "Security and peace of mind are at the top of the list to most folks today, and I would imagine that the peace of mind from the security offered in our neighborhood is important to you, isn't it?" (They won't say "No").

YOUR PRODUCT

Script 10 specific features you want to spotlight, generally in this suggested order:

1. The first feature should be a statement about the architectural design, land plan, variety of floorplans and homes you have to offer.
2. The second item should be a statement about your customer service department and warranty program. It is a fact that people today are very concerned about what's going to happen with them after they move into their new home, so before they see the first model, they should understand that you are a company who cares about their long-term satisfaction and will stand behind that commitment.

3. Item three should be a statement about financing.

   Wouldn't you agree that it is important for someone, before they even see the first model home, to have a good understanding that they can afford to own it? It can be as simple as this:

   > "Mr. and Mrs. Jones, we have a variety of financing programs available for most folks — both fixed rate and adjustable rate — so I'm sure that we have a plan to fit your needs."

Primarily, as part of item number three, you don't want your prospects to be thinking, as they walk through the model homes, "This is really nice, but we can't afford this." Dispel their negative thoughts.

Items four through ten should be those product features and benefits which you feel are the most important in the homes that you offer: from an energy efficient heat pump to hardwood floors, and from top-of-the-line appliances to walk-in, cedar-lined closets.

As you explain product features and benefits, don't forget to use brand names. People are impressed when you mention General Electric, Whirlpool, Frigidaire or Kenmore appliances. Carrier, Rheem, Ruud — these are air conditioning names that people recognize immediately. If you use Johns- Manville or Owens-Corning Fiberglass insulation, don't hesitate to state those names. People even distinguish such names as Kohler or Briggs in connection with plumbing fixtures. These companies spend millions to convey brand name recognition to the consumer. Tap into that free publicity.

Remember, a home is nothing more than the sum total of all its component parts which are crafted together by a builder who cares. You have already told the prospect about your company's history and customer service program; now you want to spotlight the component parts.

With two of the products, use appropriate tie-down statements, especially as you recap:

> "Our homes contain 17 inches of fiberglass batting in the ceiling. As a matter of fact, we use the finest insulation from Owens-Corning. That's going to provide you with a tremendous sense of energy efficiency and savings. I would imagine, like most of the folks I talk with, that energy efficiency is important to you, isn't it?" (Once again, they won't say "No").

Consider the following outline.
Look at the vital elements you must cover.

*THE FIVE MINUTE DRILL*SM

HOW TO ORGANIZE AND LEARN THE NECESSARY INFORMATION FOR A QUALIFIED, PLANNED PRESENTATION

Directions: Use The Five-Minute DrillSM Outline to organize your facts. Then write a narrative script using them to convey your Five Minute Presentation. Recite it out loud as many times as necessary to perfect it. Record your best presentation.

I. **ME/MY COMPANY** (Approximately 45 seconds)
   A. Who are we?
   B. What have we done?
   C.* What does that mean to them?

II. **LOCATION** (Approximately one minute and 15 seconds)
   A. General (Macro-The Area)

	Feature	**Benefits**
1.		
2.		
3.		
4.		
5.*		

   B. Specific (Micro-The Neighborhood)

1.

2.

3.

4.

5.*

*Indicates use of an appropriate "tie-down" or involvement question.

THE FIVE MINUTE PROFESSIONAL
(continued)

III. AMENITIES (approximately one minute and 15 seconds)

	Feature	Benefits
1.		
2.		
3.		
4.		
5.*		

IV. THE PRODUCT (approximately one minute and 15 seconds)

	Feature	Benefits
1.		
2.		
3.		
4.		
5.		
6.		
7.		
8.		
9.*		
10.*		

NOTES:

A SAMPLE FIVE-MINUTE PRESENTATION

"C'mon, Bob," you chide, "how do you put all that information into five minutes? There's no way." Let's do it!

A nicely dressed man has just walked into your sales office. He is obviously in a hurry. You greet him. He says, "I'm Joe Jones. I'm moving into the area soon with my wife and two children. Right now, I'm on my way to the airport, but I wanted to run by here and pick up a brochure and other printed materials about your houses and development. Have you got something handy for me to take back home to the wife and kids?"

"Sure, Mr. Jones," you reply. "Let me put together a packet of literature especially for you. Do you have a few moments for me to do that?"

"Okay," he says. "But no more than five minutes at the most."

"That's perfect, Mr. Jones. Welcome to the XYZ Community. While I'm putting together this packet for your family, allow me to tell you quickly about my company, Great Homes of America. Based here in Central City, we are a company of long-standing integrity and quality. We've built a number of well-known communities throughout the state, including ABC and DEF."

"Great Homes is a member of the National Association of Home Builders, and has, for over a quarter of a century, built quality homes for more than 50,000 wonderful people. (Note: people, not families). We are considered one of the largest home builders in the state. Our success is a result of construction quality, the value we offer, and the integrity and financial stability of Great Homes."

"Since 1967, in addition to planned communities and neighborhoods, Great Homes has built some of our state's large office parks, including our corporate headquarters in Central City."

"As a new owner of one of our homes, Mr. Jones, you will be assured of a pledge to stand behind a quality-built and affordable home—one you and your family would be proud of."

"The experience, integrity, financial stability and accessibility of the builder of your new home would be important to you, wouldn't it?"

("Sure," he answers to your first tie-down, giving a green light for you to continue. You have been talking for 45 seconds. You move ahead confidently to spotlight your location.)

"Now, about our neighborhood — Great Homes and our special homeowners feel that the south section of Center City is one of the finest locations you can enjoy."

"You mentioned that you are on your way to the airport. That 20 minute trip would sure be convenient, wouldn't it?"

(That's tie-down number two and the end of your macro-location features and benefits. Go ahead to the micro-location details.)

Also, we have a vast array of shopping centers, churches, banks, restaurants, recreational facilities — all within five minutes. Won't that save time?

(That's three tie-downs, so far.)

"Our school system is excellent. Ms. Brown, the new principle of our elementary school just invested in the XYZ community, and she is a delightful neighbor."

"Let me mention as a bonus, in the XYZ community, you only have county taxes, which is about 25% to 30% savings. I'll bet you could find plenty of things to spend your money on beside taxes, am I right?"

(Tie-down number four. Plunge into the amenities.)

"And even though we are in the county, this neighborhood has city water and sewer, curbing and guttering and all underground utilities. And everybody loves our colonial reproduction street lamps."

"I notice that you are fit. We have a jogging trail, lighted tennis courts and an olympic-size pool — all here for you and your family to enjoy."

"A feature of our neighborhood, which sets us apart from the subdivisions and tracts you may have already seen, is what we call protective covenants. These help maintain the nice appearance of the neighborhood. Can't you imagine how these protective guidelines help maximize your investment, rather than seeing it destroyed by uncaring neighbors?"

(Tie-down number five)

"Other homeowners agree wholeheartedly with you!"

(Charge into your product. Mr. Jones is warming!)

"Now, since you have a very limited time today, which keeps me from showing you each of the floorplans, let me share a few features of our homes which should interest you."

"First, Great Homes is so confident of our quality and workmanship that we offer a one-year builder's warranty, plus an insured warranty program, at no additional expense. This would protect you against any major structural problems that might come up."

"By the way, during those 10 years, your homeowners policy is transferrable to subsequent owners. All of our XYZ homes have Rheem water heaters, Carrier heat pumps, and each carries the energy efficient rating."

"All these features, don't you agree, would save you money and make your family's home more comfortable the year around?"

(The sixth tie-down)

"Additionally, each home has two and a half baths. You can have three or four bedrooms. You will enjoy a custom-crafted deck, an impressive all-brick fireplace, Anderson tilt-out windows, a finished two-car garage and your choice of brick or lap hardboard-siding exteriors."

"These are all nice features, don't you think?"

(Tie-down number seven...You are cooking now! Mr. Jones is giving very positive body language. Finish your product features and benefits with a flourish.)

"One last point I'd like to mention is that Great Homes has a positive, long-standing relationship with many of the finest lenders. We can offer you very attractive financing. In addition, we pay all allowable closing costs and discount points."

"Presently we are offering a conventional 30-year mortgage or an adjustable. Our financing enables you to take what you would normally apply to closing costs, and you can use it as part of your initial investment. That would represent a substantial savings to you, wouldn't it?"

(That's tie-down number eight. You have less than a minute left. Recap the complete presentation.)

"Now, Mr. Jones, I told you rather quickly how conveniently located XYZ is to the airport, to shopping and recreational areas. Wouldn't you agree this is a great location for any family?"

(The ninth tie-down)

"And you were pleased to learn that your tax bill would be substantially less than if you lived inside the city, weren't you?"

(Number 10)

"Just from what you have said about yourself and your loved ones, the features about the home that I have mentioned would be pleasing to your family, wouldn't they?"

(Eleven tie-downs)

"And don't forget the attractive financing that XYZ has put together through lending institutions. That seemed to interest you, didn't it?"

(That's 12 tie-downs. Look at your watch and smile. Your entire presentation took just under five minutes!)

May I ask you this. Of what you have seen today of our homes, which one do you think you like the best? ...

PUTTING YOUR SCRIPT TOGETHER

You can do even better! So much of the sample script had to be generalized. With your details, you can put together an impassioned, knock-out presentation.

Fill in the blanks with your basic information, then go back through your outline and make your first pass at the FIVE-MINUTE DRILL. The first few scripts may be more than five minutes, but with some rewriting and condensing, you can get it down under the allotted time.

By the way, did you notice on the outline that the total time allotted for presenting the four ideas is actually four minutes and 30 seconds?

Why?

If you get **ME/MY COMPANY** down to 45 seconds, and **LOCATION, AMENITIES and PRODUCT** each down to one minute and 15 seconds — a total of four minutes and 30 seconds — you automatically have an edge with the typical "just looking," "on the way to the airport" or "Grandma is in the car" prospect who gives you five minutes.

Prospects are floored when they issue you the "five minute" challenge, hear your dynamite material presented and then have you look at your watch. "Well," you say, "we only have thirty seconds left. I would sure like to show you our model homes. . ."

I have found that buyers are sometimes liars. When you do a tremendous FIVE-MINUTE PRESENTATION, you will be surprised at the large percentage of "gotta run" people who suddenly start signaling, "Tell me more!"

Why get your script down to four minutes and 30 seconds? It is that *"slight-edge"* mentality that increases your presentation-to-closing ratio significantly.

"SLIGHT-EDGE" GOALPOSTS

This is a slight departure from new home sales, but allow me the privilege, since I am a diehard professional football fan.

I used to wonder how the great field-goal kickers could appear to be so calm during those gut-wrenching moments with their team down by two points and less than five seconds left in the game.

Can you imagine being so focused that you can ignore 80,000 screaming fans, a worldwide television audience, your pacing coach, the multi-million dollar contracts and 11 massive, opposing players who would love to stomp you into the plastic turf? Somehow the great kickers are able to block out the pandemonium, have their feet make perfect impact with the football and watch it sail neatly between the 18-foot wide goalposts 30, 40 or 50 yards down the field. It is utterly amazing, requiring the style of an artist, the flawlessness of an engineer and the courage of a mercenary!

When some kickers display this ability during the game, what you don't see is the reason why they can be so calm, precision-like and professional.

A former pro football kicker, Bob Unruh, and now a top professional new home sales manager, told me that his kicking coach developed a special practice goalpost. Instead of allowing the normal 18 feet between the two uprights, the practice apparatus was only 14-feet wide. Each week he and others used this narrow goalpost.

Far from the crowd, they rehearsed for the big moment. They kicked hundreds of times during the week without anyone watching except the center and the person who holds the ball.

But mentally, they heard the crowd's thundering roar. They watched the snap and placement. They kick it perfectly. They mentally saw the scoreboard flash three more points. It's the same thing over and over again. The rehearsal is even more mental than physical.

When they are summoned onto the field during an actual game, the kicker knows he is prepared. He closes his eyes and runs through the motion. He tells himself, "I've been through this thousands of times. I've been kicking hundreds of these this week through the narrow goalposts. This one is a piece of cake through the wider uprights!"

What does this mean for you in the new home sales arena? Script a four minute and 30 second presentation. Practice. Drill. Rehearse. Get ready for the big moments.

Under those narrow limitations, an actual presentation that may run as much as 30 minutes or more will be a breeze by comparison. Practice your script hundreds of times. Sure, you will improvise. Of course, it will run more than five minutes in many real-life situations. But when you are ready, lean and mean, nothing can faze you. It all comes down to scripting and PDR.

After all, compared to the kickers, isn't your career as important? Aren't the stakes equally high?

A FINAL NOTE

Write our your FIVE-MINUTE PRESENTATION in long-hand, then go back and read through it. Analyze every word. Evaluate every statement. Whittle and redesign. Make sure it is absolutely the best presentation you can make.

Then tape yourself. Record it over and over until you are comfortable with your presentation. Get so good that you have trouble remembering it came from a script.

Please understand, I do not believe in *canned* presentations or scripts in the marketplace. I do believe in scripting your presentation to organize your thoughts and Practice-Drill-Rehearse.

Once you learn the script, say it anyway you want. If your product is more impressive than your amenities, put the product section first. If your location is especially exciting, spend more time on it and less on your amenities.

I will say, however, that if you have scripted and learned your FIVE-

MINUTE PRESENTATION well, you can stay very close to that script and still flow naturally and dramatically.

Mainly, remember that this is a *drill.* It is an exercise. It is organizing the information in order of priority. It is a super-confidence builder.

Once prepared, you are the master communicator. Why should you panic? "You only have five minutes?" you can say with a pleasant smile. "Great. I'm glad you stopped by. . ."

If you can frame your presentation from a position of strength, you will convey your orderly, organized information with confidence. When you are confident, you will never be intimidated. Eleanor Roosevelt said, "No one can make you feel inferior without your consent." Confidence builds trust. Trust translates to closings. Closings. . .well, you get the general idea!

In Chapter Ten, you will learn how your FIVE-MINUTE DRILL fits into your overall planned presentation.

1. Be ready for "I just have a moment to look" opportunities by preparing a Five-Minute Presentation.

2. Your FIVE-MINUTE DRILL includes sections on ME/MY COMPANY, LOCATION, AMENITIES and PRODUCT.

3. Practice, Drill and Rehearse your scripted FIVE-MINUTE PRESENTATION.

4. Condense your presentation to four minutes and 30 seconds for *"slight-edge"* confidence.

Chapter Ten

SHOWTIME!
Your New Home Sales "Main Event"

"One of the things about acting or painting or writing
or composing music is you never get it right.
You can spend a lifetime, and, if you're honest with
yourself, never once was your work perfect.
People say to me, `You've got the awards and the
parts and the money. What are your goals now?"
I say, `To get it right one time.'"

—CHARLETON HESTON

SHOWTIME!

A hush fills the room. The drum-roll throbs as the curtain rises. A spotlight spills across the stage, illuminating the central character. This is it — the "Main Event!" It's SHOWTIME!

But — new home salesperson — you are not the main character. You are not bathed in the spotlight.

You are the scriptwriter, producer and director. You set the stage. You control the tempo and mood. You must create solutions to last-minute snags. You motivate your actors and make compromises with temperamental stars. You run the show.

Perhaps opening night reviews do not run in the *Times* or *Variety*, cries of "Author! Author!" do not ring throughout your performing center and Hollywood is not calling for movie rights. Maybe you are not besieged by admiring fans nor do *Entertainment Tonight* reporters stand in line for your latest quip.

But it is SHOWTIME! nonetheless. If you are good at what you do, even 5% better than your competition, your performances will be a smash at your local bank and you will enjoy a long-string of hit sales presentations!

SIX STEPS TO THE SEQUENCE FOR SUCCESS TO NEW HOME SALES

In the FIVE-MINUTE DRILL, you were shown how to organize and script the basic information which you need to convey.

But scripted monologues do not a standing ovation make! Staging, pacing, framing — there are so many additional elements which can transform your excellent script into a multitude of successful sales.

In this chapter I will show you how to stage and highlight that presentation.

Earlier I discussed some of the differences between the average salesperson and the highly-paid professional. One point: The average salesperson will not stand in the way of a transaction taking place, but the professional causes the transaction to happen and knows — every step of the way:

What happened?
Why did it succeed or fail?
How did I cause the result?

The *"slight-edge"* professional has an organized presentation, a singleness of purpose and understands how to maintain control while appearing to be natural and conversational.

With the FIVE-MINUTE DRILL, you are learning how to organize your information logically, sequentially and dramatically.

What I want to help you to do is take that information and learn how to expand it into a presentation that might take 30 minutes or longer. In fact, a complete and proper on-site, new home sales presentation — from greeting to the close/follow-through — could take upwards to one hour or more. To keep a prospect interested for that length of time requires a very structured, practiced performance.

I will sometimes refer to the complete process as your PLANNED PRESENTATION, and I will also call it the SEQUENCE FOR SUCCESS TO NEW HOME SALES. Both titles refer to the same strategy.

There are six scenes in your SHOWTIME! process:

GREET
QUALIFY
DEMONSTRATE
SITE/SELECT
CLOSE
FOLLOW-THROUGH

Here are a few "memory pegs" to help you remember this vital outline for your PLANNED PRESENTATION.

Hold up the hand you write with, put up your thumb and say **GREET**.
Hold up your forefinger and say **QUALIFY.**
Add the next finger and say **DEMONSTRATE.**
Next, the ring finger and say **SITE OR SELECT.**
Raise your little finger while saying **CLOSE.**
Then make a fist and say **FOLLOW-THROUGH.**

Use whatever techniques you need, but remember that this is the order you should always use. You can use flexibility when it comes to each component, but you should never change the basic six-part SEQUENCE FOR SUCCESS of your PLANNED PRESENTATION.

Now, let's go through each scene of your "Main Event" SHOWTIME! performance.

Remember, Mindset #1. Before you make any presentation, ask yourself, Who am I, Where am I and Why am I here.

GREET

During the first few moments, you want to establish trust and make a friend. You DON'T want to plunge immediately into a "pitch." (CANCEL-CANCEL!)

Remember that people enter your sales office filled with fear and fragmented feelings. Warmly offer your hand and say "Welcome to XYZ!"

Avoid "May I help you?" or "What can I do for you?" Trite, redundant phrases label you as an amateur. Also, unless your company insists, avoid "Could I get you to sign in?" or "Register please" greetings.

If you are on the telephone when someone comes in, put your conversation on hold, get up, greet the prospect and then excuse yourself with the promise to be right back.

One of the best ways to get people to respond positively to you is to offer them a non-alcoholic drink. Make it hot in the winter and cold in the summer. A drink establishes a hospitable, homey atmosphere, and subliminally it helps obligate the prospect to you. Little touches can make big *"slight-edge"* differences!

While getting the prospect a drink, you can begin qualifying without appearing to be regimented or pushy.

Remember that your "Main Event" SHOWTIME! begins when the prospect enters the door. The spotlight goes on him, her or them. The prospects are the actors — let them be the center of attention. You are the producer/director. Your task is to maintain control and put together a rousing success.

QUALIFY

Your purpose in qualifying the prospect is to determine who the person is, what he or she really needs and how you can fill that need.

Your ability to close will be in direct proportion to how well you have learned to qualify. Why? You cannot close properly until you know enough qualifying information about the prospect.

The qualifying process technically begins after the greeting; in actuality, it continues throughout your presentation and overlaps every other step.

Some new home sales offices use a printed prospect card or form-sheet for determining the needed information. Others use a less-formal three-by-five card. Whatever method you use, try my C.O.M.M.A. format. I introduced this acronym earlier. Let me explain how it will work for you:

COMMITMENT — **Is the prospect serious?**

You can't come right out and ask, "Are you serious?" So, you want to structure your C.O.M.M.A. questions — Colombo-like — in such a way that you can get all the qualifying information you need. You must be conversational, not nosey or tacky. (Warmth and sincerity goes a long way toward believability).

One question you can ask to determine commitment is this:

"Is this your first visit to our model center?" or "Is this your first visit to XYZ Community?"

If they have been there before, you want to know if they have talked with one of your associates; also, a second or third visit indicates the possibility of more interest than somebody who might be "just looking" for the first time.

Another question: "How long have you been looking at new homes?"

If the answer is "We have been looking for some time," then begin your "just looking" qualification. Find out what they have seen and especially what they liked. Listen to the responses intently, for they may come right out and divulge specific WII-FM? "hot buttons."

If the answer is "Oh, we've just started looking," simply say, "That's great. I'm just curious, how many new homes or model communities do you think you will have to look at before you find the one that really fits your needs?" Whatever they say, ask, "Could you describe the features and benefits you're looking for in a new home?" More "hot buttons!"

The "first visit" and "how long" questions are the only two you generally need to determine commitment.

OPPORTUNITY --- **What does the prospect need and want?**

As you have learned, there is often a significant gap between the message/want and the meta-message/need. Many times people will say what they want is a four-bedroom, three-and-a-half bath home with a three-car garage, swimming pool and tennis court --- on 10 acres next to the country club, no less! What they really need is a nice 3/2 with a one-car garage on a 70-by 100-foot homesite. If you do your presentation trying to place the family in the estate, rather than the nice home, you are inviting disappointment on the part of all concerned.

Question in terms of need, size and opportunity: "What type home are you looking for?" or "Could you please describe for me once again some of the features you want in your new home?"

Also, alternative choice questions work well: "Do you need two or three bedrooms?" or "Do you prefer a one-or two-story home?"

MOTIVATION --- **Why is he or she here?**

The prospect could be anywhere else on the planet, but he or she has driven out to your model home center. Think about that!

Also, people who are shopping for new homes have dozens of other places they could look. Your competition's billboards, magazine/newspaper advertisements and broadcast commercials seek to attract the prospect's attention.

But he or she is with you. Why? As soon as you can answer that question, you uncover vital "hot buttons", and obtain buying motivation clues.

Ask, "How did you happen to hear about our community?" Whatever they say (advertisements, a friend, a Realtor, a sign, or just driving by), ask, "What in particular in the ad (or what was mentioned that) attracted your attention?"

Be quiet and listen. They may uncover WII-FM? signals that you would have never received otherwise. When the prospect gives an explanation, discuss the reasons for a moment, perhaps elaborate, and then inquire, "Was there anything else?"

More "hot buttons!"

The sooner you can tune in to the WII-FM? signals, the better you can tailor your presentation to the prospect's most important needs.

MONEY — **Does the prospect have the financial ability to invest in a home?**

You want to determine if he or she is financially capable or qualified to own one of your homes should they like it.

"Do you have a $150,000 in the bank?" is a bit crude. There are, however, questions which you can ask to obtain financial information.

Say, "Our homes range in value from $__________ to $__________. Is that basically what you had in mind?"

You can also inquire, "Do you currently own or rent?" If rent is the answer, find out when the lease expires. You may not completely define an ability to purchase, but you can determine urgency.

If they own, probe deeper: "Will you be selling your present home before you acquire a new one?" Find out if it is currently on the market, its price range and prospect activity.

One more point: If the prospect owns a home, ask, "What type of home do you own now?" Listen to the answer, then continue: "That sounds like a lovely home. What do you like best about it?" Also, you can play the dream-maker: "I'm just curious, if there is anything about your present home that could change to make it ideal for your present situation, what would that be?" Answers I have heard include: "It's too small/large. It's not energy efficient. I want a larger kitchen. I wish it was closer to my job." Whatever reasons are offered are generally the best "hot buttons" you will receive.

ACTION — **When will the prospect act? When will he or she decide?**

Assuming you show the prospect something that he or she likes and desires, when will the decision be made?

We can no longer afford to do business as usual. Let me explain. Today's buyer is much more aware and in many ways more sophisticated than any buyers in past times. Old "pushy" questions or tactics that were once somewhat effective no longer work. Unfortunately, some of those are still being taught. One glaring example that immediately comes to mind is this; "If you see a home that you like, are you in a position to make a decision now or in the near future?" On the surface, this might sound o.k., but in my seminars, I ask all attendees, "How many of you have ever heard this technique and been told that it would work, or have been taught to use it?" Most often, (depending on the length of experience selling) many hands will go up. Then, I ask, "o.k., you have heard it taught, how many of you use it regularly?" Without exception, no hands go up. "Why?" I ask. The answers are always the same. "It's corny, too pushy" and so forth. I like to teach real world communication skills that work. By changing the words slightly and positioning them from a "pushy" yes or no question to a gentle, open ended probe, we increase the probability of a positive response greatly.

Instead, say this: "Mr. and Mrs. Jones, when you find the home that you really like, when do you think you would be moving in?" Most will say, "Oh, when I sell my home" or "in two months."

Whatever they say helps qualify them, especially in terms of action.

How and when do you ask the C.O.M.M.A. qualifying questions? As mentioned, the sooner you have the information, the better you can tailor your presentation. However, don't jump all over the prospect in the first few minutes if they are not ready. You can qualify *throughout* the PLANNED PRESENTATION.

Remember that selling is an *art* and a *science.* I can help you with the science. I can offer suggestions for your Practice-Drill-Rehearse sessions. But you must develop your artistic qualifying ability in the actual marketplace.

With some people, you can ask the questions systematically, one after the other, and they have no reservations about giving you plenty of valuable information. Others may show a body-language roadblock, so you may have to phase your questions over a longer period of time.

Remember I explained that people are subconsciously looking for reasons NOT to purchase a new home, even when they visit your model home center. Therefore, the qualifying process may involve more than just determining needs or wants. If your company has a wide variety of homes or if you have a prospect who is very unspecific or non-responsive with his or her answers, you must use a bold, qualifying move which will help you gain information, in a reasonably short period of time, about what their interests are.

For example, you say, "We have homes from the mid-eighties to the $300,000 range — what are you most interested in seeing?" Or, "We have a variety of floorplans, all the way from one bedroom to four bedrooms. What would you like to see?" If they reply, "Oh, I don't know — I'd like to see them all," use this strategy: "That's great, Ms. Jones. I know I'm going to enjoy showing you through all of our models and floorplans. About how much time do you have? (They will tell you, thereby making a commitment.) Usually, the answers will range from about ten minutes to about 45 minutes or an hour. When they commit, then say, "it will take approximately (state the longest amount of time that it would effectively take to show "everything") to show you everything we have to offer. With that in mind, where would you like to start?"

You will be surprised how specific they get! Your strategy, when you are genuine and friendly, quickly helps them to put the situation in proper perspective.

Above all, the new home sales "Columbo" loves a challenge. Be prepared. Know the C.O.M.M.A. formula backward and forward. As the producer/director of your SHOWTIME! "Main Event," you must know the scripted lines so well that you can improvise and maintain control, no matter what the "actors" do.

DEMONSTRATE

Generally, you demonstrate by showing your product, building emotion, asking questions, listening carefully and observing the prospect's responses.

Specifically, as outlined in Chapter Nine's FIVE-MINUTE DRILL, you want to show your product from the outside in: you and your company first, the micro- and macro-location next, then the amenities and your product.

Based on the material in Chapter Nine, you can give a dynamite presentation in less than five minutes, right?

But you generally don't have to reduce everything to those limits. Ideally, you can expand your presentation to a much longer time as you move through your "props."

You have many "props" or tools available to you. Most sales offices have an array of wall displays, graphs, aerial photographs, maps and interior photographs. Every company provides brochures, floorplans and materials. You generally may have one or more model homes

The average new home salesperson considers these tools as *the presentation*. You know better. The tools are merely "props" for your carefully crafted PLANNED PRESENTATION.

Since the tools are not the primary focus, you can use them more confidently to "dress up" your presentation. For example, if you have a large aerial map of the community or a display panel that spotlights your company, use it to point out specifics during the COMPANY or LOCATION part of your presentation.

When showing your model homes, have a planned and rehearsed course of action. Sure, you can be flexible, but know in advance what you want to highlight.

Start with the outside. As you walk toward the model home, point out three or four key features of the outside (paved drives, covered front porch, landscaping, lighting, trees); you should be able to establish positive factors even before you get inside.

As you enter the home, remember that you should never point out more than three features in any room. Know those three specific items in advance. The only exception is the kitchen — it is such a central room that you may want to mention six or eight features. Also, on the subject of central aspects, don't forget to focus on bathroom features.

If a room is small, such as an extra bedroom, don't walk into the room with the people. Stay in the doorway and allow them to enter the room.

In larger rooms — the master suite or den — walk away from the prospects to the opposite side. Move around casually. These strategies emphasize the extra space.

Here is one *"slight-edge"* demonstration secret: Get so specific and descriptive that a blind person could take a tour with you and be able to understand *everything* in your presentation!

Paint vivid word-pictures. Don't call it "a fireplace" it's a "cozy" fireplace. Don't just call the home "new," talk about being able to select colors or use a creative tie-down, "I just love the smell of freshness in a new home, don't you, Mrs. Jones?" Point to the patio and remark, "Won't you enjoy entertaining your friends on this magnificent flagstone terrace?"

Use lots of tie-downs during the demonstration stage. Show and test. Ask questions.

SITE/SELECT

In this step, you actually take prospects to the physical location, or locations, which would be available for them to build their home. Or you take them to specific homesites or completed residences which are available for immediate ownership. Plan your driving to go past the most interesting features of the community. If possible, avoid muddy roads or heavy construction areas. Choose the most scenic route.

If possible, park your car on the opposite side of the street from the homesite or completed home — it gives a panoramic view. It also gives you those few moments to point out the three external features as you walk.

If they are interested in a specific homesite, get them to walk on their future terra-firma. It helps establish ownership. Have their preferred floorplan with you, and talk specifically about the exact location where the home will be situated. Say, "Mrs. Jones, with this floorplan, we would be standing in your den and looking through those french doors into your backyard, wouldn't we?"

Don't hesitate to show them a number of homesites, but a general rule is three or less during a visit.

Again, use alternative choice questions: "Of the three sites you have just seen, which one do you like best?" (Then, SHUT UP!) Or, "Do you prefer the cul-de-sac homesite with the huge oak tree in the backyard, or the location nearer to the tennis courts?" (Again, SHUT UP!)

CLOSE

I will spend most of SECTION FOUR dealing with objections and closes. Suffice it to say that your primary goal is a mutually-satisfying conclusion to the PLANNED PRESENTATION.

Specifically, you should explain the purchase procedure and ask for the sale. Do the paperwork. Overcome objections. If you do not close, establish a firm follow-up appointment.

FOLLOW-THROUGH

The new home sales industry places such emphasis on "props" and high prospect volume that sometimes the *"Follow-Through"* step is diminished and neglected. In Chapter Fourteen, I will spotlight the entire spectrum of being persistent, following up on "be-backs" (CANCEL-CANCEL), creativity and after-sales service.

Do you want a concise outline of the PLANNED PRESENTATION points? Use this practical guide:

SEQUENCE FOR SUCCESS COMPONENTS

This is a specific outline of individual activities within the SEQUENCE FOR SUCCESS TO NEW HOME SALES. It is intended as a guide for putting together your professional presentation.

I. THE GREETING AND APPROACH

A. I will introduce myself when greeting the prospect and obtain his/her name.
B. I will determine:
   1. The number of visits to the sales office.
   2. What attracted them to my community.
C. I will be neat and professional in my appearance.
D. I will be polite and enthusiastic.

II. THE QUALIFICATION

A. I will qualify the prospect using the C.O.M.M.A concept, and will ask:
   1. The size of family.
   2. Type of home desired.
   3. Price range desired.
   4. Type of home moving from.
   5. Reason for moving.
   6. Time needed.
B. I will determine:
   1. Employment status.
   2. Ability to purchase (cash or mortgage).

III. THE DEMONSTRATION

(This information is contained in your Five-Minute Drill.)

A. PRESENTATION
   1. I will discuss myself/my company.
   2. I will conduct the tour of:
      a. Information center.
      b. Models.
      c. Homesites or available completed homes, if applicable.
      d. Recreation area.
   3. I will take control when touring models and homesites.
   4. I will have a PLANNED PRESENTATION and conduct it in a professional manner.

B. COMMUNITY KNOWLEDGE
   1. I will discuss:
      a. quality of the neighborhood.
      b. residents.
   2. I will offer information on:
      a. schools.
      b. shopping.
      c. hospitals.
      d. churches/synagogues/temples.
      e. recreation.
      f. transportation.

C. SPECIFIC AMENITIES/PRODUCT KNOWLEDGE
   1. I will discuss:
      a. variety of available homes.
      b. sizes/floorplans/types.
      c. quality of individual homes.
   2. Key features and options.
   3. Financing and lending institutions.

IV. THE CLOSE

A. I will offer the procedure for purchase.
B. I will ask for the sale.
C. I will ask for the sale more than once.
D. I will show an agreement.
E. I will fill out an agreement.
F. I will attempt to overcome objections.
G. I will establish a firm follow-up appointment.

V. I WILL OBTAIN A COMPLETE PROSPECT REGISTRATION CARD.

(This may be accomplished any time before or after the presentation.)

ADDITIONAL POSITIVES:

A. I will ask, "What in particular in the source (ad, sign, friend, etc.,) attracted your attention?"
B. Each time the prospect uses a negative word, I will feed back a positive "power" word.
C. I will properly use a minimum of six tie-downs during the presentation.
D. I will feed back every objection the prospect raises.

DETRACTING NEGATIVE:

Each time I use a "negative" word, except when used to discuss the competition, it detracts from my overall effectiveness.

A FINAL NOTE

As a new home salesperson and professional communicator, you are also the producer/director of "the best show in town" when the "actors" walk into your sales office. Why should you be so concerned with the dramatic element of your PLANNED PRESENTATION?

1. Everything you do as a salesperson — your preparation, "props" and livelihood — is reduced to the "moments of truth" when you come face-to-face with each prospect. If your "Main Event" isn't memorable, someone else's will be.
2. A "SHOWTIME!" mentality gets the prospect's attention and interest.
3. Dramatization increases the customer's understanding of your company's reputation, as well as the features and benefits of your location, amenities and product.
4. A "Main Event" PLANNED PRESENTATION is more convincing than a mediocre, babbling "pitch."
5. Dramatization makes a more lasting impression. You lay the groundwork for the prospect's future visits and your *"Follow- Through"*.

Remember, in terms of your SEQUENCE FOR SUCCESS PLANNED PRESENTATION, the values of your product and your competitor's product are perceived as being equal by the customer unless someone explains the difference. Plus, you and your company are no better than your most marginal competitor, unless you have the ability, know-how and pizazz to sell and interpret the difference.

During each "Main Event," spotlight every feature and benefit as though it were exclusive. In a very real sense, if your competitor fails to match your presentation, yours IS exclusive in the eyes of the prospect!

It's SHOWTIME!

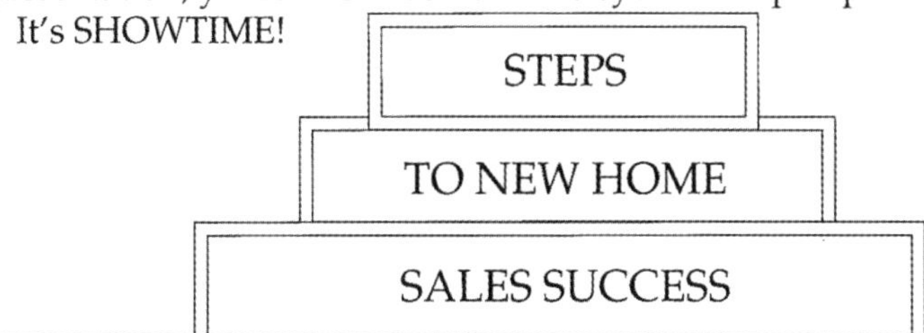

1. It is SHOWTIME! when the prospect walks into your sales office. You are the producer/director. The customer is your actor. Spotlight him or her!

2. Your PLANNED PRESENTATION should follow this SEQUENCE FOR SUCCESS: GREET, QUALIFY, DEMON-STRATE, SITE/ SELECT, CLOSE and ***"FOLLOW-THROUGH"***.

Chapter Eleven

THEY HAVE TO *OWN* IT BEFORE THEY'LL *BUY* IT

"In selling, your product has got to have differences that are perceived and real. You've got to fill a niche. You've got to point out the differences as a plus. . . you've got to have an angle, a twist, a point that differentiates you and then you've got to make the most of it."

—MALCOLM FORBES
Owner, Forbes Magazine

INVOLVEMENT

Someone has said, "Uneducated people are SOLD, but smart shoppers BUY." In the new home sales industry, you can have a comfortable lifestyle SELLING people your product and taking orders. But to join the *"slight-edge"* ranks of well-paid professionals, you will be required to help each prospect BUY. The difference is much more than semantics.

Certainly the pre-sold, first-visit people do come into your model home center. If your marketing and advertisements are superior, sometimes as high as 15% of the prospects who come into your sales office are willing and ready to look over your options, complete the paperwork and write a check.

The bulk of your sales are more difficult, requiring several visits, more objections, site/selection wavering, multiple closes and consistent, well planned *"Follow-Through"*.

All new home salespeople can handle the first group. Furthermore, the commission check from the "easy-sell" spends just as well as from the more difficult closes.

The average salesperson learns to deal effectively with the second group, the more difficult customers.

Only a few, perhaps 5% of the new home salespeople, begin moving into the marginal, extra-hard sells. You have to earn the right to close people in this group.

What makes the difference? As discussed throughout the book, there are many *"slight-edge"* factors. One of the most useful can be summed up in two words: CUSTOMER INVOLVEMENT.

When they own a home psychologically, they will buy it physically. The difficult part is getting prospects to that point.

"COLOMBO" QUESTIONS

I spent most of one chapter talking about questions. Questions help you guide the prospect toward becoming a satisfied customer. For the new home sales "Colombo," there are seven basic question types:

FACTUAL — to get information — "What, where, why, who and how?"
EXPLANATORY — to get additional information or broaden the discussion — "How would this help?"
JUSTIFYING — to get proof or to challenge old ideas and get new ones — "What makes you say that?"
LEADING — to introduce a thought of your own — "Would this be a possible solution?"
HYPOTHETICAL — to use assumptions or deductions — "What would happen if we did it this way?"
ALTERNATIVE — to get a decision or agreement — "Which of these floorplans do you like best?"
COORDINATIVE — to develop common agreement or to take action — "Do we all agree that this is our next step?"

The secret is to use questions which bring the prospect closer to an emotional investment. Learn Colombo's secret well and master the art of asking creative questions, getting people to like and trust you, helping people open up and posing questions in such a way to get the answer you desire.

You should especially become a professional at offering an alternative of choice — "Do you prefer a one or two-story home?"

TIE-DOWN QUESTIONS

Tie-downs can fit into any of the above types, and they can be one of the finest tools you can use in your trade. I suggested using a minimum of six in your FIVE-MINUTE DRILL. Expanded into your six-part SEQUENCE FOR SUCCESS PLANNED PRESENTATION, you have an opportunity to use dozens of tie-downs.

Why use tie-downs?

1. **Tie-downs help the prospect experience ownership.**
   The skillful use of tie-downs helps keep the prospect involved in your presentation and point toward emotional ownership.

Here are tie-down examples:

Hasn't he?	Hasn't she?
Won't they?	Won't you?
Aren't they?	Aren't you?
Shouldn't it?	Wouldn't it?
Haven't they?	Couldn't it?
Can't you?	Doesn't it?
Don't you agree?	Don't we?
Isn't it?	Isn't that right?
Didn't it?	Wasn't it?

2. **Tie-downs help you maintain psychological and emotional control of the presentation.**
   Recognize that when you are taking a prospect through your PLANNED PRESENTATION, he or she has many other things in mind — grocery shopping, getting to the airport, Grandma who is still out in the car. Therefore, the prospect may miss the beautiful entranceway or the architectural designs of your model homes, even though they drove right past them.
   Tie-downs can make the difference!

3. **Tie-downs help cement a prospect's belief.**
   This point goes much deeper than getting the prospect to experience the "props" you offer.
   If you state *anything* about your company, the location, amenities or product, it is automatically subject to doubtful review by your prospect. After all, that is your job. You are the salesperson, and your job depends upon painting rosy pictures about the homes you want to sell.
   However, if you can get the prospect to say the same thing or verbalize agreement with your statement, it instantly becomes more believable.

FOUR TYPES OF TIE-DOWNS

Once you learn to use tie-downs properly, you must also develop a variety of ways to use these tools. Let me suggest four basic variations:

1. CONCLUSION TIE-DOWNS
   Used most commonly, these involvement phrases are used at the end of a statement:
   "The view from this balcony is lovely, *isn't it?*"

2. INVERTED TIE-DOWNS
   These phrases are used at the beginning of a statement: "*Wouldn't it* be convenient for your children to be able to walk to school?"

3. INTERNAL TIE-DOWNS
   Sometimes involvement questions can be used in the middle of a statement: "Mr. and Mrs. Jones, as we stand where your own flagstone terrace and swimming pool will go, *can't you* imagine how you and your family will enjoy a cool dip in that pool on a hot summer afternoon?"

4. TAG-ON TIE-DOWNS
   When your prospect volunteers a positive statement, use the op-

portunity to add tie-down words to cement and highlight the thought. For example, suppose your customer says, "These cabinets sure are beautiful." Smile, nod and warmly add, *"Aren't they?"*

Make sure that you use tie-down statements and questions wisely. Be careful that you only pose them in such a way that logical people will give you a positive response. Don't use "the view from the balcony" tie-down, for instance, if you are standing on a homesite which has a terrible view. If you do, you deserve to have the prospect retort, "Actually it isn't a great view — it's horrible!"

ONE STEP AT A TIME

You see, as you establish psychological control and move the prospect toward emotional ownership, you want to get the person to agree with you on a lot of little points.

Get people to respond positively to you, beginning with your greeting: "Hello! It's great to have you here. It sure is a beautiful day, isn't it?"

Skillfully, use dozens of tie-downs during your PLANNED PRESENTATION. (Remember, warmth and sincerity, not glib or flippant). Help people feel good about agreeing with you.

Numerous small agreements combine to make one big close! That's what you want.

A FINAL NOTE

There is one major danger with tie-downs. There is the saying, "A little education can be dangerous." A person with a little knowledge of tie-downs can also be dangerous.

You may say, "Wow! Tie-downs are great. I'm going to start using them." But two weeks later, if you are ending every other statement with ". . .don't you agree?" your presentation will become even more dull and monotonous than before.

Variety is the key.

Basketball star Michael Jordan has the sweetest 15-foot, fall-away jump-shot in the National Basketball Association, but he takes that shot sporadically. Instead of putting up one 15-footer after the other, he uses a vast arsenal of shots — charging lay-ups, breath-taking slamdunks, under-handed flips and mid-air eye-poppers.

Why? Michael Jordan does not enjoy "eating" the basketball! You see, there are five players on each opposing team, at any moment during any game, who would dearly love to "jam it" back down Michael's throat. Few players can boast about doing that to the star forward.

You also face people who would enjoy "blocking your shots" during your presentation. Predictability — in basketball and new home sales — can be both monotonous and dangerous. Variety is the key to effectiveness and artistry!

Become a master at asking questions. Use tie-downs for involvement and for a much higher presentation-to-close ratio. Determine to join other *"slight-edge"* professionals who have learned this secret!

1. Uneducated people are SOLD, but smart shoppers BUY.

2. Your prospect has to OWN the home before he or she will BUY it.

3. Tie-down questions help your prospect establish emotional ownership, assist you in maintaining psychological control of the presentation and cement the buyer's belief.

4. Use variety with four types of tie-downs: CONCLUSION, INVERTED, INTERNAL and TAG-ON.

Chapter Twelve

HOW TO HANDLE OBJECTIONS PROFESSIONALLY

"The biggest block to personal communication is man's inability to listen intelligently, understandingly, and skillfully to another person. This deficiency in the modern world is widespread and appalling."

—F. J. ROETHLISBERGER

MORE INFORMATION, PLEASE?

"It's too much."

"I think I'm gonna wait awhile before buying."

Anytime a prospect offers resistance, it is great! Objections indicate interest. Never be unhappy with turndowns.

In the new home sales industry, objections are usually requests for more information, and they take five "hidden" forms:

1. **A need for rationalization.**

   Sometimes an objection can be a cry for help. Deep down, the prospect probably agrees with you on every point that you've made, but he or she wants to be a bit more convinced that the investment is wise, safe and not extravagant. Price objections almost always fit into this "hidden" reason.

2. **A desire for ammunition and support.**

   The first "hidden" reason related to an inner compulsion to obtain more information for one's self.

   This reason is similar to number one, but it centers on the need to get more support material to help convince others — family, associates and neighbors — who will question the investor's decision.

   Whether they say it or not, everyone knows that a major decision, such as a new home purchase, invites a barrage of opinions and challenges:

   "You did what?"

   "You should have bought so-and-so!"

   "I would have waited awhile."

   Nearly everyone is surrounded by "Monday morning quarterbacks" who believe it is their calling in life to second-guess everyone who makes a major decision about a new car, a career move or a different hairstyle.

   It is your job to give prospects more than enough "comeback" ammunition for their know-it-all friends, relatives or associates.

3. **A request for reassurance.**

Deeper than either of the previous reasons, this need springs from a natural nervousness shared by most people. Any rational person wants to be absolutely certain that they are making the best decision — one they won't regret.

When a prospect resorts to foot-dragging and stalling, don't take their maneuvers personally. If you have positioned yourself as a caring professional, prospects probably mistrust you less than they trust themselves!

When they put up barriers, all they may be asking you to do is go over the reasons again to convince them that they are making the right decision.

4. **A matter of pride.**

The prospect may be totally convinced that you are the best salesperson, your community the finest and your homes the most wonderful. As a matter of pride, however, he or she may feel obligated to "deal" or stall.

An objection, especially a lower-price challenge, is probably an attempt to "feel you out." Let's face it, most prospects think, "What have I got to lose?"

As a new home salesperson, you have an established, firm price, so you usually cannot negotiate. Your job is to focus on quality, helping the prospect understand that he or she is getting a great price for an even greater value.

5. **An attempt to "blow smoke."**

Sometimes people just like hearing themselves talk. Other people make silly statements just to throw you off-guard.

In the middle of your presentation, you may get a prospect who says, "Oh, I see you don't paint the inside of the air-conditioning grill."

Or, the person may suddenly look up at a skylight and remark, "Wow! I wonder how in the world you could ever clean that?"

Both actually happened to me. "Blowing smoke" objections should be treated as serious as other reasons. How do you know what is important to the prospect?

You can never take objections at face value. You must search for the meta-message which is obscured by the turndown. If you understand the "hidden reasons" for what they are, you will be in a better position to say the appropriate thing and move into a successful close.

When you take the objection literally and give up, you not only lose the sale, but you do a monumental disservice to your customer. If he or she really needs and wants a new home and you don't close, some other salesperson will complete the transaction.

HANDLING OBJECTIONS

Objections may come throughout your presentation, but they will usually explode as you move into the closing step. (The more you close, the more objections you will raise). Consider these ideas with regard to a prospect's objections:

1. **Objections help eliminate or minimize questions in the prospect's mind.**
   The closing process invites lots of objections. Your goal is to systematically eliminate or minimize any negatives.
   If you have more answers than they have objections, you will probably gain more of their attention and eventually close.

2. **You can use objections to do more qualifying.**
   "Hot buttons" are often obscured by turndowns and negative statements. Probe deeper for the WII-FM? signals.

3. **You must be totally prepared for every possible objection.**
   Preparation breeds confidence. Confidence invites trust. Be overly prepared to refute turndowns with an amazing variety of features, benefits and emotion-getting statements.

THE MILLION-DOLLAR LIST

In the FIVE-MINUTE DRILL, I asked you to put together at least 10 features and benefits for your company, location, amenities and product. You should be in the process of learning that list through many Practice-Drill-Rehearse sessions.

Now, let me get you to compile a list of 20 specific objections. There are three groups of objections you can use: the ones you have heard personally, the ones you are waiting to hear and the ones you would raise if you were the customer.

You may want to brainstorm with others in your sales office. Get *very* specific.

Using the steps explained in the remainder of this chapter, develop planned answers to those objections. Many may require research about your company, location, amenities or product, but your payoffs for that diligent effort will eventually translate into commission checks!

Many, many times, you will find that there will be more than one answer to the same objection. That's quite common. You may even have two or three different answers that will overcome or minimize a similar type objection.

Take that list of objections and answers, and put them in the order you feel they will be raised most frequently. Number them, and then memorize these objections and their answers. You should be able to answer each objection without even thinking about it. You will then be "unconsciously competent."

If you are totally comfortable and prepared, when someone raises an objection during the presentation, you will never be caught off guard.

This list may change from time to time, as your market or location shifts, but the principle itself will stay intact.

By the way, you may not be able to be eliminate some objections. If so, script answers which will minimize them. For example, if there is a sewer plant near the entrance to your community (Heaven forbid!), it might be a bit difficult to get rid of the problem. You can, however, minimize its impact by building the value of your other features.

Please do not skip this step! Take the time to list your objections and answers. Prioritize and number them. Commit them to memory. P-D-R! This one step, by itself, can be worth thousands in saved, marginal sales.

MASTER THESE STEPS TO OVERCOME OBJECTIONS

When a prospect raises an objection, they mention it because they want to say something. Their words may or may not be significant.

If someone raises an objection, even if you have the perfectly prepared answer, you may not want to immediately shoot down their objection with your gem. Just giving the answer itself is not always the best response.

Think about the selling situation as a tennis match. Player A serves the ball to the other, which becomes the stimulus of the tennis game — the cause that starts the action. Player B, on the other side of the net, has to make an instinctive decision as to what to do, where to be and how to return the ball. When that happens, Player B pauses for a split-second, makes a decision and attempts to return the volley. If Player B hits it successfully, that" thunk" causes Player A to pause, decide, and respond. The process will go back and forth until one of the players does not pause/decide/respond correctly. For lightning-quick Steffi Graf or Boris Becker, the PDR seems effortless and flowing. Although naturally gifted, both Graf and Becker are incredibly wealthy because they have successfully returned zillions of volleys, first in practice and later under a worldwide spotlight.

In new home sales, you must become the Steffi Graf or Boris Becker of objection-returning. Every time the prospect raises an objection, he or she is serving the "ball" to you. You must pause/decide/respond to return the volley. If you are successful, the prospect must do whatever he or she can to hit the "ball" back. Again, you pause/decide/respond. This goes on, as in a tennis match, until one of you misses the "ball."

Become more prepared and proficient in this process. When you understand what is happening as it takes place, you can become a PROactor, not merely just a REactor. Also, you will discover super-confidence and mental agility.

Here are six basic steps for you to use in the objection process:

STEP 1: Hear the objection out.

Far too many new home salespeople pounce on the turndown statement before the prospect gets the words out. No only does this interrupt and irritate the customer, but it makes you look pushy and unprofessional.

Be calm. Listen with empathy and understanding. People like to hear themselves talk. Give them the opportunity to express their concerns and emotions without constant interruptions.

STEP 2: Feed it back.

This is a critical point! This strategy often helps the prospect answer their own objection as they hear it spoken back to them.

Repeat the objection *word* for *word*. In an inquisitive fashion. Remember Colombo's technique.

When the prospect says, "The bedroom is too small," say, "The bedroom is too small?" Do it just like that.

This step has four obvious benefits:

- It makes your prospect feel important.
- It verifies the objection.
- It gives you a micro-second to pause before you respond. Be relaxed, and they will never know that your mind is whirring through your arsenal of answers.
- When you repeat their words, often the prospect will see that the objection is superfluous. Your feedback may answer the question.

Feeding the objection back works especially well as you deal with couples. Many times I have fed an objection back to the prospect, only to have the spouse answer the objection immediately and begin to close for me! It works.

Also, often you can feed the objection back with good information: "Let me make sure I understand, Mr. Jones. Essentially, you say you really like everything about our home and the homesite you've picked out, but the backyard is not exactly what you're looking for?" By feeding an overwhelming positive with the objection, you help the prospect put the entire picture in perspective. Often Mr. Jones will say, "Well, considering everything else, the backyard isn't that small."

I have found that in 20%-30% of the time, feeding the objection back will cause the objection to be answered. The secret is to practice feeding the objection back with warmth and sincerity, and with a slightly curious tone in your voice.

If the objection is eliminated or sufficiently minimized by feeding it back, go into a close. Otherwise, if the objection persists, move into the third step.

STEP 3: Question the objection.

Ask the prospect to elaborate. Use Colombo's line: "I'm curious" or "Can you elaborate on that?" Ask, "Mr. Jones, what do you mean about the backyard — do you feel it's too large or too small?"

Avoid any hint of sarcasm, impatience or condescension. Those emotions reveal that you are out of control, and you will probably lose the sale.

Be serious and curious. Get to the basis of their objection. When the meta-message is revealed to them, they will often remove it themselves.

If not, while the prospect is answering your question, you will have a moment to prepare for their next volley.

STEP 4: Answer the objection using your pre-planned responses.

Let's be honest — one of the reasons I have asked you to work so diligently on your features, benefits, objections and answers, is because I have never seen a perfect community. Even the best planned neighborhoods have some weak points.

Don't volunteer the information, but if a prospect raises a firm objection about one of your weak points, if you have studied painstakingly, you have one or more answers already prepared.

Don't run from strong objections. Use them. Probe. I have found that you can uncover a gold mine of "hot buttons" in this step if you maintain control while showing sensitivity, warmth and empathy.

Make a comparative advantage statement: "Mr. Jones, I can understand and appreciate that, but let me point this out . . ." Without admitting your weakness, you build your case with stronger features and benefits.

If your prospect accepts your answer, move to step five. If he or she raises the same objection, go back through steps one through four and pinpoint the exact problem. Then go on to step five.

STEP 5: Confirm the answer.

Don't overcome the objection, then leave it hanging in mid-air. Even if you were completely clear in your mind, the prospect may not have heard or understood what you covered.

After you answer the objection, confirm the fact with a concluding tie-down. Ask, "That's the answer you were looking for, wasn't it?" or "That makes sense, doesn't it?"

If the prospect doesn't understand or agree, you are better off knowing right then. Why let the "unanswered" objection fester? If the prospect isn't satisfied, redefine by going back through steps one through five before moving ahead.

If the prospect nods or verbally agrees, move on immediately to the next step.

STEP 6: Move on!

If the objection has been answered satisfactorily, don't wait around for it to come back to haunt you. Shift gears. Use Colombo-like transition words: "Oh, by the way. . . ," "Would you follow me?" or "Wait until you see this!"

The concept is to avoid getting hung-up on objections. Objections are slight detours to the professional who uses the "SEQUENCE FOR SUCCESS" and has a planned presentation.

ONE ALTERNATIVE TO REMEMBER: Shelve it!

One option, especially when an objection is raised during the early- to mid-portion of your presentation, is to shelve it.

There are occasions when it is not to your advantage to confront an objection. For example, let's say you are demonstrating the first of four model homes to Mr. and Mrs. Jones, and you have not yet shown the amenities — such as recreation facilities — which will cause the couple to get involved in your community.

Suppose in the initial model home, Mrs. Jones steps into the very first bedroom and says, "This bedroom is just too small!"

Sure, you could hear the objection out, feed it back, question the objection, answer the objection using your pre-planned answers, confirm the answer and move on.

But in that situation, you would probably be better off to listen to the objection and say, "Mrs. Jones, I can appreciate that, but what I'd like to do is to show you the rest of this home, the remainder of our community, and then, if you'd like to, we can come back over here and I'll get a tape measure to see if your furniture will fit. That will be okay, won't it?"

Since I have learned the shelving technique, I've found that nearly 100% of my customers go along with my suggestion. More importantly, at least 75% of those shelved objections are forgotten or answered during the course of the presentation.

Unfortunately, I didn't always know this strategy. There really was a Mrs. Jones who made the "too small" remark in the first bedroom she viewed, and instead of doing what I would do now, I immediately got a tape measure and graph paper and set about to prove that she could get all of her bedroom furniture into that room.

No, I didn't close that Mr. and Mrs. Jones. But I did learn that you can make a fatal mistake in "majoring in the minors." So, when you feel that the time is inappropriate or too early for your Mr. or Mrs. Jones to raise an objection about interest rates, wall coverings or 1,000 other subjects, just shelve it.

Again, remember that warmth, sincerity and curiosity are absolutely necessary to deal with objections using these steps.

TWO CONDITIONS FOR LOSING A SALE

Faced with objections and failure, the mediocre salesperson finds an *excuse*. Successful new home salespeople find a *way!* Nido Qubein, the well-known consultant, speaker and educator says, "When you are a professional, you must accept a higher level of responsibility."

Part of your obligation, if you are going to serve your customers professionally, is to guide prospects through their uncharted waters by eliminating or minimizing objections.

An *objection* should never stop the customer from buying a new home. Only a valid condition should stop a sale, and there are only two conditions which a *"slight-edge"* professional can accept:

1. No money
2. No credit

Anything but those two conditions is an objection. For the best salespeople, if no *condition* exists and they do not invest in a new home, *you must accept the responsibility!*

A FINAL NOTE

Learn to love objections, because they point the way to closing a sale. When you deal with objections effectively, your customers BUY their home, rather than allowing you to SELL it to them. Objections help your customers to become more involved, and more closings will come naturally as you become proficient.

Vince Lombardi, legendary coach of the world champion Green Bay Packers, used to say, "We have never lost a football game, although occasionally the clock runs out before we get more points on the scoreboard than the other team does. But we never lose a game."

Lombardi was one of the winningest coaches in the history of the National Football League. Why? The Packers played five quarters during practices, not the normal four periods. During the games, the players were mentally prepared to outlast anybody. When the opposing team began wearing down during the final quarter, the Packers only got better.

You must be overly prepared to win the objections game. More than ever, you have to be willing to do the unexpected and extra, to join the ranks of highly-paid, *"slight-edge"* professionals.

Remember: pause/decide/respond. With the growing list of answers to objections which you are amassing, you are bound to become one of the best!

1. Objections from a prospect are usually requests for more information.

2. Be prepared by putting together your "Million-Dollar List" of the 20 most-asked objections and your prepared answers.

3. Learn to handle objections by using the six basic steps: HEAR THE OBJECTION OUT, FEED IT BACK, QUESTION THE OBJECTION, ANSWER THE OBJECTION USING YOUR PRE-PLANNED ANSWERS, CONFIRM THE ANSWER and MOVE ON.

4. There are only two conditions which a professional will accept for a missed close: no money or no credit.

Chapter Thirteen

A DOZEN POWERFUL CLOSES FOR NEW HOME SALES

"Closing is selling!"

—TOM HOPKINS
Master Sales Trainer

ALWAYS AIM TOWARD THE CLOSE

You have learned six PLANNED PRESENTATION steps to be used in new home sales: **Greet, Qualify, Demonstrate, Site/Select, Close and Follow-Through®.**

As the quote above says, "*Closing is selling*!". Some powerful closes created by Tom Hopkins that are perfectly appropriate and applicable to new home sales, and therefore included in this chapter are the Secondary Question Close, the Lost Sale Close, and of course, the New Ben Franklin Close. These, together with the other closes that I have created, will give you a tool box of essential closing strategies to heighten your new home sales effectiveness.

As a new home salesperson, you must recognize a vital truth -- the first four steps point toward the close. The final stage depends upon the close. Your entire presentation must always aim toward the close.

Why? Selling without closing is like acting without applause. Without a successful close, apart from the two conditions I have mentioned -- no money or no credit -- you have failed.

By definition, there should be a number of "closings" within the framework of your PLANNED PRESENTATION. You can use tie-downs, trial closes and questions which progressively add up to the major close. But unless you ask for the sale and complete the purchase agreement, you fail yourself and your prospect.

If closing is your weak-link, take heart. Let me share some principles and strategies! These are "trench-tested" in hundreds of model homes -- closing techniques which you can begin using immediately.

NEW HOME CLOSING PRINCIPLES

When I asked inexperienced or average salespeople what bothers them most about their profession, 98% of the time they say something to this effect:

"Closing makes me so nervous."

"I do fine until I have to get out the paperwork and start asking them to go ahead."

"Almost all the time, even with the most cooperative, willing buyers, when I talk about the purchase, I tense up, I can see them tensing up. It's the part about selling new homes that I really hate!" Oh, I don't ask closing questions until they indicate they are ready to buy."

---

1. Follow-Through® is a registered trademark of Hoffacker Associates.

If you are bothered by the close, you are not alone. Psychologists cite "closing stress" as an emotion which is shared by nearly all salespeople, in varying degrees. Psychologists also generally agree on the cause: FEAR OF REJECTION. You must never take their NO, personally.

Consider this antidote. The most beautiful girl on the campus (the home coming queen) is often not asked out on Saturday night, because all the guys are afraid she will say "no"! Then you see her one weekend at a party with a "Quasi Moto" look alike. You ask him, "How did you get her to go out with you"? "Easy" he says. "I asked her." Weren't you afraid she would say no?" "Heck no, he replies, they all say no, so I thought I would start with her."

Maybe you would be surprised to learn that your prospects EXPECT to be closed. Many, if not most, of them actually WANT to be closed. Every new home investor depends on a salesperson who has expertise and knowledge. They want to deal with a professional who can help them obtain a new home.

A new home close is a win-win situation when both the investor and salesperson get what they want. When you offer a legitimate proposal, they recognize your professionalism. But when you show a lack of expertise, the prospect detects that, too. Therefore, it is the prospect's duty to look for flaws in your presentation and proposals.

Customers must satisfy themselves that your company's quality and service are acceptable before they will consider your price. Many will not approve the paperwork until they are convinced that they have your best offer.

"Best offer" does not necessarily mean the lowest price. It does mean the best price for the quality and service the customer wants and expects to receive.

When there is an agreement on the features and benefits the customer desires, he or she expects you to close. When you hesitate, they begin looking for other flaws.

Don't disappoint your customers. Offer solutions, then close! *Always attempt to close at least three times during your PLANNED PRESENTATION.*

Here are several closing points to remember:

1. Your prospect remains a prospect until he or she meets a professional closer.
2. Your closing savvy rests in your ability to help people make decisions which are good for them.
3. If you can't close, you can't sell.
4. The sale is made in the presentation, but it is lost in the close.
5. Closing means meeting the prospect's urgency and need with your product.
6. You must find the prospect's WII-FM? signal and "hot buttons" in order to close.

Remember that the close is your systematic elimination or reduction of all the prospect's objections. Above all, you must earn the right to close!

BE PREPARED TO CLOSE ANYWHERE, ANY TIME

I was in the fourth year of selling new homes, in my early twenties, top salesperson month after month for the largest builder in Florida, and, considered myself an overall hotshot. When a new vice-president of marketing was appointed to the company, a man brought in from California, one of the first things he did was say, "I'm going to have each of you salespeople evaluated by the use of `shoppers' who come through your model homes and go through your presentations with a hidden tape recorder."

I was miffed. After all, I was the company's "top gun." How could the new VP *dare* question *my* sales ability?

The company was so convinced that the new executive could take us to a new performance level that they used an effective close on me: "Do what we say or go work for the competition."

Infallible logic! Considering the fact that I didn't want to work for our competition, I decided to go along with the "shopper" idea. After all, I was a hotshot, but I wasn't stupid.

When I got my first shopping tape back, I was absolutely amazed at how horrible my presentation was. For starters, I heard immediately that I was one of "those salespeople" who merely engaged in a conversation. I paid little attention to the customer's buying signals.

Part of the way through the tape, as we went through the first model home, I heard the shoppers indicate their interest: "We really like this floorplan."

I retorted, "Well, if you like this one, you're really going to like the next model. It's our best seller!"

I had a lot of other problems, but the worst was the fact that I had put myself at the center of the presentation. The prospects were "bit" players.

More than that, I hadn't yet learned one major concept:

> THE "*SLIGHT-EDGE*" PROFESSIONAL IS ALWAYS PREPARED TO CLOSE ANYWHERE, ANY TIME AND UNDER ANY CIRCUMSTANCES!

In addition, I learned then, which is why I stress it so much today to my students, that taped shoppings as a learning tool are the most sure fire method for those dedicated to achieving greatness to achieve it.

Learn today what it took me several years to discover. Close the sale when the prospect is ready. In fact, a great time to close is while you are demonstrating the product. At that time the prospect's emotional level is at its peak. Therefore, don't hesitate to close in the model home.

Your goal is to build value to the point that the prospect is ready to close. Whenever that happens, stop selling and close! Don't overkill.

To do this, always carry a legal size binder which contains a purchase agreement, calculator, and any other information necessary to close.

CLOSING IN YOUR OFFICE

Every company is unique in the sales office set-up. Regardless of your office configuration, consider these guidelines:

1. Your desk and work area should always be neat, organized and clean.
2. If possible, use a round closing table rather than a desk.
3. During the close, avoid distractions and maintain your prospect's rapt attention. Try to have the person face a blank wall.
4. Never allow the telephone to interrupt you while closing. If working alone, disconnect, put it on hold or use an answering service or machine.
5. Never interrupt or disturb an associate when he or she is in the process of closing.

One final note, in order to eliminate or minimize the fear of shock, put your agreement (the paperwork) on your closing table *facing the customer.* It should be an integral component of the natural selling process, not a mysterious, hidden document.

A DOZEN POWERFUL CLOSING STRATEGIES

Generally, all closing strategies fall within a dozen techniques. Certain ones will work better for you than others, but you should have all of these maneuvers in your "tool chest:"

1. **The Trial Close**

   When you feel that the prospect is generally agreeing with you, ask a trial question — "Which floorplan do you prefer, the ABC or DEF?" Always be ready to move from a trial close into the major agreement.

2. **The Question-with-a-Question Technique**

   Anytime a prospect asks a question, seek to answer that inquiry with one of your own. Write down the answer. Be ready to move into the close.

   For example, when someone asks, "Can I get a kidney-shaped pool?" Ask, "Do you want a kidney-shaped pool?"

   If he or she says "no," you would be foolish to spend time selling them on this point. Maybe the person hates kidney-shaped pools and doesn't want to live in the same neighborhood with one. Move on.

However, if the person says, "yes," you can say, "Let me make a note of that," then ask a trial close to see if the kidney-shaped pool was the clincher.

3. **The Alternative Close**

Tied to the alternative question which should be used throughout the PLANNED PRESENTATION, this close offers a choice, either of which may result in purchase agreement. Here are 10 of the best alternative close questions:

- **Carpet installation** — "Would you like us to install your carpet by the first or fifteenth?"
- **Move-in date** — "Would you prefer moving in on the first or the fifteenth?"
- **Cash or mortgage** — "Would you like the agreement to read 80% or 90% financing?"
- **Site location** — "Would you prefer to move into the corner location we looked at or the home on the cul-de-sac?"
- **Recreation location** — "Would you want to build your home on the lake or the golf course site?"
- **Exposure location** — "Would you prefer to move into the residence with the southern or the northern exposure?"
- **Legal** — "Do you want the agreement to be drawn in one name or jointly?"
- **Walk-through inspection** — "Since your decision is made on the location, would the first or tenth of February be better for your walk-through inspection."
- **Bank-credit interview** — "Since your decision seems to be made, would you like me to set the bank interview for next Monday or Wednesday?"
- **Financing Plan** — "Having made the floorplan selection, would you prefer the agreement to contain the 15-year or 20-year financing plan?"

4. **The Summary Close**

Use this technique in combination with other closes. Say, "Let me summarize what we have talked about to this point. You like the ABC floorplan. Now, which homesite do you prefer for your home, 17 or 31?"

Remember that your major close is a collection of smaller ones.

5. **The Secondary Question Close**

Ask the major decision question, and without pausing, ask a minor question that they can easily answer.

For example, say, "As I see it, the major decision we have this afternoon is when you and your family will begin enjoying your new lifestyle at the XYZ community. (Don't pause!)By the way, do you want the oak or walnut cabinets?

. . .80% or 90% financing?

. . .the kidney- or rectangular-shaped pool?

When they give you an answer to a minor close, subconsciously they also acquiesce to the major close.

6. The Erroneous Conclusion Close

Sometimes, especially when you have developed a very friendly relationship with the prospect, and when you feel a need to help the prospect define needs and to propel him or her toward the close, you can purposely make an erroneous statement about something you know that they decided upon and have previously confirmed to you.

Try this: Even though the prospect has let you know that they want the kidney-shaped pool, homesite 7 and the oak cabinets, summarize by saying, "Now, Mr. and Mrs. Jones, let me make sure that my notes are correct. You want the oval-shaped pool, homesite 7 and the oak cabinets. Right?"

"No," Mr. Jones replies, "everything you said is correct except the pool — we want it kidney-shaped, remember?"

"You're right," you quickly admit. "I see it now on my notes. Please forgive me."

The prospect cements the close with his or her own words.

7. The New Ben Franklin Close

The great J. Douglas Edwards first taught this close, and it has been later refined and taught by such legendary trainers as Tom Hopkins.

When the prospect absolutely wants to own the new home, but needs help in making the decision, say this:

> "History has proved that most great decision-makers believed that a good decision was only as good as the facts. The last thing I would want to do is to influence you to make an unwise decision. "However, if it proves to be a good decision, you would want to make it, wouldn't you? Fine. Do you mind if I help you?" (Don't pause.)
>
> "Let's draw a line down the middle of my legal pad and on this side list the facts favoring the right decision today, and then over here list the reasons against the decision.
>
> "When we are through, we will count up the columns and at that point make the right decision. Let's see . . ."

You then list all the reasons for going ahead. Go for at least six reasons. Then you turn the pad around to them, hand them the pen and warmly say:

> "Now, let's see the reasons you feel are against the decision."

Be absolutely quiet. After they are through, say, "Well, let's see what we've got." Add up both columns and say, "Now, that settles that, doesn't it?"

"By the way," you add, "this decision-making device was created by the great Benjamin Franklin and we've all considered him one of our wisest men, haven't we?"

8. The Take-away Close

This close works best when a prospect wants something which is in short supply (Example: specific homesites). If you know, for example, that the prospect wants the remaining homesite near the tennis court but are playing coy games, say this:

> "Mr. and Mrs. Jones, I believe that you really like this homesite with its beautiful view, closeness to the tennis courts and (re-state other features and benefits). But since you may not make up your mind today, I have a suggestion that will help you avoid being disappointed later.
>
> "As you know, this is the only available homesite near the tennis courts. In case someone else decides to invest in your favorite homesite before you do, let's pick out another one *almost as nice.*" (Remember, shut up.)

If the prospect is serious, he or she will take mild offense at your suggestion and say, "We don't want something else *almost as nice.* We want that one near the tennis courts."

Remark, "Great!" Move into the major close.

(P.S., I know a *"slight-edge"* professional who used this one within the first week after learning it in my seminar to close a $650,000 sale!!)

9. The Similar Situation Close

For prospects who have no valid conditions for not going ahead but are hesitant because of price, use this comparison technique, emphasizing FEEL, FELT and FOUND (tailored to your specifics):

> "Folks, I know you FEEL very concerned about making this decision. I must say three months ago, I talked with a nice couple like yourself who had the exact concerns.

"The Taylors had waited five years to own a home, living all that time in an apartment and paying rent. We talked about why they wanted to move here and they FELT their main reason was that they wanted their children to be raised in a nice home and a safe neighborhood.

"After considering their children's happiness, and the financial benefits, they FOUND they had no significant difficulty investing.

"I know you both FEEL the same way, don't you? Would you prefer. . .? (Close!)

10. The Pulley (not Pushy) Close

Prospects often say, "We want to think it over." If you have done everything correctly in your presentation and earned the right to close, the "think it over" statement may only be a stall.

Say this:

"I can appreciate that, Mr. and Mrs. Jones. Obviously you wouldn't take your time thinking this over unless you were seriously interested, would you? (You want a new home?)

"I mean, I'm sure you're not telling me that you want to think it over just to get rid of me, are you? (Again, another no.)

"So, may I assume you will give this investment very careful consideration?

"Just to clarify my thinking, what phase of this opportunity is it that you want to think over? (Don't pause.) Is it the quality of the service I and my company will render? Is it (give two or three more positive statements with which you know they will agree)? Is it something I've forgotten to cover?

"Seriously then, please level with me. What is it that you want to think over? (Be absolutely quiet.)

If you receive no response, suggest inquisitively, "Could it be the money?" If they nod or agree verbally, handle that objection by reducing the money factor to understandable terms. Then begin closing again.

11. The Order Blank Close

If everything seems agreeable, take the paperwork, poise your pen and ask a reflex question which can be given without thinking: "Mr. Jones, let me make sure of the spelling for your first name. Your middle initial is? What is your street number?"
Keep writing and asking reflex questions until they stop you.

12. Lost Sale Close

When it seems hopeless that the prospect will make a decision, use this technique. Sadly pull the paperwork back toward you and ask for the person's help and clarification:

> "Ms Jones, before you leave, let me apologize for not doing my job well today. You see, if I had done better, I would have said and done the things necessary to convince you of the value of our homes. Because I didn't, you and your family will not be among those who enjoy the benefits of our beautiful homes and our community. Believe me, I am truly sorry.
>
> "Ms. Jones, I believe strongly in our community and earn my living helping people enjoy it. So that I don't make the same mistake again that I've made with you, can you please tell me, what I did wrong?"

Listen intently. Take notes. Listen for missed "hot buttons." Through the years, I have closed at least 50 "impossible" prospects with this "Lost Sale Close" because I took one more opportunity to listen and pick up on a person's WII-FM? signals.

There you have them — a full dozen of the best, most effective new home sales closing strategies. Learn them all. **Practice-Drill-Rehearse** until you achieve a *"slight-edge"* professionalism.

POSITION THE PAPERWORK

Eventually the agreement comes down to paperwork. For starters, use a *"slight-edge"* pen — at least a Cross or Schaeffer. Invest in a Mont Blanc, if possible. Don't insult your customer by asking him or her to approve a $150,000 purchase agreement with a 50-cent pen.

After completing the paperwork, turn it around, hand your pen to the customer and say:

> "Mr. and Mrs. Jones, putting together all your considerations, I sincerely feel that your decision makes good sense. With your approval right here, we'll begin your loan process (or preparing your home for occupancy)."

Smile and BE QUIET until they sign or verbalize an objection.

DON'T POSITION YOURSELF AS PUSHY

If at any time during a close the prospect says that you are getting too pushy or closing too hard, physically take a step back (lean back and relax if you are sitting). Smile to relieve the pressure. Then warmly say:

> "Okay, I'll admit that I may seem a bit too pushy. But please don't confuse my enthusiasm for my community and my sincere desire to help you and your family enjoy its benefits with being pushy. That is the last thing I would ever want to do."

Smile warmly again and immediately go back into your closing: "By the way . . ."

FINAL NOTE

Remember, just as baseball's multi-million dollar pitcher Orel Hersheiser or tennis' Steffi Graf cannot be too prepared, neither can you. And if your SEQUENCE FOR SUCCESS PLANNED PRESENTATION depends on anticipation of the prospect's "volleys," your closing-stage preparation is even more imperative!

CLOSING, AFTER ALL, *IS* EVERYTHING!

1. Always aim toward the close.

2. Prospects expect a professional to close, so always attempt to close at least three times during any presentation.

3. Be prepared to close anywhere, any time.

4. Learn all 12 closing strategies and be thoroughly prepared to use any one or a combination to bring the presentation to a mutually-satisfying agreement.

Chapter Fourteen

THE "MAIN EVENT" CONTINUES

"If you have only one idea, you have only one course of action open to you, and this is quite risky in a world where flexibility is a requirement for survival."

—ROGER VON OECH, Ph.D.
President of Creative Think

FOLLOW-THROUGH, THE *"SLIGHT-EDGE"* DIMENSION OF CLOSING

"Follow-Through" is not an add-on feature; rather, it is a can-do attitude which should permeate your sales presentation from beginning to end.

If you are not genuinely interested in serving people, that attitude will show, no matter how well you think you have hidden it.

Even if you have put together a monumental PLANNED PRESENTATION and have developed a closing style that would rival Zig Ziglar's, unless you really care about the long-term benefits of your prospects and customers, you will never reach the heights of success that you could (otherwise) attain.

Where does caring and a *"Follow-Through"* attitude begin? By way of explanation, let me repeat "The Ten Commandments of Customer Relations," a classic collection of truisms which has been passed around in sales circles for years.

Here are 10 points which can move you into a higher dimension of new home sales:

1. **The customer is never an interruption to your work.**
   The customer is your real reason for being in business. Let other tasks wait!
2. **Greet every customer with a friendly smile.**
   Customers are people, and they like friendly contact. They usually return it.
3. **Call customers by name.**
   Make a game of learning customers' names. See how many you can remember. This is a valuable habit.
4. **Remember — you are the company!**
   In the customer's eyes, you are as important as the president of your company — probably even more so.
5. **Never argue with a customer.**
   The customer is always right (in his or her own eyes). Be a good listener, agree where you can and then do what you can to make that person satisfied.

6. **Never say "I don't know."**
   If you don't know the answer to a customer's question, say, "That's a good question. Let me find out for you."
7. **Remember that the customer pays your wages.**
   Every dollar you earn comes from the customer's pocket. Treat him or her like the boss, since that person indirectly signs your paycheck.
8. **State things in a positive way.**
   Choose positive words when speaking to a customer. It takes practice, but it is a valuable habit that will help you become an effective communicator.
9. **Brighten every customer's day.**
   Make it a point to do something that brings a little sunshine into every customer's life, and soon you will discover that your own life is happier and brighter.
10. **Go the extra *("slight-edge")* mile!**
   Always do a little more than the customer expects you to do. You will be richly rewarded during your life for this habit. (Incidently, I have found that very often, the "extra mile" is a very lonely stretch of highway).

Whether your prospect invests in your community or walks out without approving the paperwork, you must find a way to be a *"slight-edge"* new home salesperson.

These "Ten Commandments of Customer Service" form the foundation for effective *"Follow-through"*.

BE-BACKS

Remember when you used your fingers and hand to help you memorize the six steps of the SEQUENCE FOR SUCCESS PLANNED PRESENTATION. The final step, with the words emphasized by your fist, was *"Follow-Through"*. The fact that this word is imaged in your closed hand is no accident. When you become a great *"Follow-Through"* professional, that hand will be filled with multi-figure commission checks.

Your follow-through begins with "be-backs." I know that this is a negative, CANCEL-CANCEL word. That is still true. Don't use it in the model center. In this book, however, which is written specifically to help new home salespeople, "be-backs" is the best term to describe a prospect who visits your community more than once before deciding to invest.

Your "be-back" business is vital! Despite your desire to close every first-time visitor to your model home, unless you have a perfect company and location which features perfect amenities and product, most of your successful closes — as much as 70%-90% — will be with "be-backs."

How do you insure a high ratio of "be-backs?" Here are several ways to *"Follow-Through"* with "be-backs" to create additional sales that would otherwise be lost to the competition:

1. **Make a dynamic PLANNED PRESENTATION on the first visit and fill it with tie-downs.**
   This should be a "given." Unless you build emotional involvement by touching "hot buttons" and tapping into the prospect's WII-FM? signal, you cannot expect a return visit.

2. **During the first visit, obtain as much information as possible to use as a basic for your *"Follow-Through"*.**
   Many sales offices have customer forms. Whether your company requires that you fill out prospect cards or not, you should devise a system to write down enough accurate information for a *personalized* follow-up: full name, address, telephone number, age, marital status, reason for wanting to move, price and urgency requirements, site/selection preferences, features wanted, names of family members who will live in the home, employment, recreational pursuits and even pets.

3. **Within two days after the first visit, send a handwritten note to the prospect.**
   Sincerely thank him or her for the visit and assure that you will call within a few days to see if the prospect and family members have any additional questions.

4. **Within a week after that first visit, call the prospect.**
   Unless he or she signals otherwise, keep the call very short. Encourage a return visit, citing a feature or two which you did not mention in the original presentation.
   Using information that you gleaned from the first visit, ask several personalized questions which have nothing to do with your neighborhood or community: "How did Junior do in the basketball game?" "How was your flight and business trip to New York City?" Then say good-bye.

5. **Keep a current catalog of prospect profile cards.**
   When Mr. and Mrs. Jones call for an appointment (or even if they show up unexpectedly), a wealth of information should be as close as your file box, Rolodex, or automated system screen.
   Also, you can use this catalog to phone or write to tell about changes: new models, added amenities or a new financing package. These simple follow-up techniques may seem simple and obvious, but they work!
   You must work, too. Effective *"Follow-Through"* strategies require a *"slight-edge"* organizational and time-management effort. Your persistence in following up every prospect will make a vital difference in your overall success as a new home salesperson.

Automated systems, like the "Handshake to Homeowner™" which we helped to develop and now market can greatly assist in a good *"Follow-Through"* program.

One additional note on this subject: Always build a genuine urgency into your "be-back" follow-throughs. Statistically, the longer a prospect waits to invest, the less likely your chances to close.

AFTER THE SALE

When you close successfully, a specific system of customer *"Follow-Throughs"* must begin. Your principal reason is two-fold — you can encourage referrals and simultaneously deal with "buyer's remorse."

Here is how:

1. **Send a personalized note (as opposed to a dreary form letter) the day after the purchase agreement is approved.**

   Welcome the customer to your XYZ family and congratulate him or her on a wise investment. Outline the next steps to be taken and reassure the customer that you and your company are committed to making sure that every step from now until closing is completed satisfactorily.

2. **Send a handwritten note to celebrate any special date which comes between the agreement and closing.**

   Remember Suzie's birthday with a cute card. Send a congratulatory note when Junior wins the state track meet.

3. **At each stage of the process — when a mortgage commitment is made, construction mileposts, pre-occupancy inspection and closing — send another personalized letter or make a telephone call.**

   You must never forget, a sale is not a sale until the final closing, and you get solid leads to other customers from them.

Every suggestion takes time. Done right, however, you will have perhaps as high as 20%-30% of your future business coming directly from referrals. Trust me, commission checks from customer referrals are extra rewarding!

CUSTOMER COMPLAINTS

Within 30-days after occupancy, continue your *"Follow-Through"* by calling to find out if there are any problems.

No matter how perfect your company may be, occasional problem situations will arise. As a salesperson whose future commission checks can be bolstered by referrals from satisfied customers, you are much better to seek out such problems than to let them fester and grow.

Use these goodwill guidelines for handling customer complaints:

1. **Be a good listener.**
   Don't interrupt. Let the dissatisfied customer get the matter completely out in the open. Sometimes when a disgruntled person exposes a "major" problem fully, it suddenly seems a bit less important.

2. **Be sympathetic.**
   Get involved. Ask questions. Show concern. Use calming statements — "I can understand why you are upset."

3. **Pay attention.**
   Make notes. Verbally acknowledge and restate their key points to let them know you understand by saying, "Let me see if I understand completely what you have said. . . ."

4. **Do something as soon as you hear about the situation.**
   Always treat complaints as legitimate and urgent. Your delay only amplifies the problem.

5. **Do what you say you will do.**
   Don't over-promise, but make absolutely sure that you *"Follow-Through"* on those things you pledge to do.
   When you can, and within reasonable economic constraints, offer more than the customer asked for or expected.

6. **Keep selling.**
   You would be surprised at the number of referrals you can get by following through on customer complaints. Done right, your action and concern can cause a deluge of "what a nice person and wonderful company" comments. Satisfied customers can translate into a prosperous network for your future sales efforts.

Above all, don't let customer complaints upset you. Have a strategy for handling them quickly and easily. The long-term benefits greatly outweigh the added time and effort required by these *"slight-edge"* strategies.

A FINAL NOTE

We all like to know that we are appreciated. Prospects who are considering an investment in a new home will be surprised and pleased to know that you appreciate their business enough to *"Follow-Through"*. Likewise, customers who are in the process of investing in your community will be delighted to know that you are not going to forget them before the ink dries on the agreement.

Remember, a salesperson's main objective should not be to make sales, but to make customers.

"Follow-Through" strategies can make a substantial difference for your short-term and long-range goals — if you are willing to be a *"slight-edge"* professional!

STEPS

TO NEW HOME

SALES SUCCESS

1. *"Follow-Through"* strategies, for customers who invest and prospects who don't, gives a powerful *"slight-edge"* dimension to new home sales.

2. Your "be-back" (CANCEL-CANCEL) business is vital, since an average of 70%-90% of your on-site, new home sales will be with prospects who visit your community more than once before deciding to invest.

3. Superior customer service after the sale can help avoid "buyer's remorse" and will encourage referrals.

4. Handle customer complaints professionally and thoughtfully.

Chapter Fifteen

MAXIMIZE YOUR LONG-TERM EFFECTIVENESS

"Most of us as individuals often act as though we think the future is something that happens to us, rather than as something we create every day. Many people explain their current activities in terms of where they have been rather than in terms of where they are going. Because it is over, the past is unmanageable. Because it has not happened, the future is manageable."

—HERBERT A. SHEPARD [1]

"SLIGHT-EDGE" PROFESSIONALS ARE PRACTICAL DREAMERS

During the first four sections of this handbook, I have outlined a number of proven strategies for reaching new home sales success. For you, the difficult part will be to believe that you can become a well-paid, *"slight-edge"* professional *before* you achieve a high level of achievement.

The problem is that the strategies don't work unless you work them. And one harsh reality is this: You will not succeed every time you try a new concept or technique. You must first become proficient, but you don't become proficient without learning through some failures.

One of life's greatest ironies is that it takes so much effort to begin any new pattern.

Just as the space shuttle burns up nearly all of its half-million gallons of fuel to lift its 74-ton cargo mere inches off the launch pad, so your aspirations seem painfully slow and unrewarding before taking shape.

With spacecraft, as in life, the most important expense, effort and mental output must take place before anyone sees results.

How do you overcome the struggles and challenges of new home sales? Here are three points to ponder:

1. **Everyone dreams and sets goals.**

   How often have you heard people say, "I just never set goals," or "I don't believe in goals. That way, I am never disappointed if I don't reach them."

   Rubbish! Everyone sets goals every day: to turn off the alarm, to get up, to eat breakfast, to go to work, to pay the bills, to watch cartoons or to run two miles.

   People have just become so accustomed to setting and reaching those everyday goals they don't recognize what they are doing.

---

1. Quoted from Taming Your Turmoil, by Peter Brill, M.D., and John P. Hayes (Englewood Cliffs, NJ: Prentice Hall, 1981), p. 102.

What if you didn't set any goals? You wouldn't get up, you would starve, you would never sell any homes, you would lose your job and the utility company would turn off the electricity. Right?

The same thought applies to your daily, weekly, monthly, yearly and lifetime goals. You are dreaming of doing SOMETHING, even if only to exist. Why not reach for the top?

2. ***"Slight-edge"* professionals, especially in the area of new home sales, have reached the top 5% of our industry because they have learned to be better dreamers and goal-setters.**

   In every field of endeavor, history's pages prove that the overwhelming majority of successful people got that way by identifying dreams/goals and following orderly paths to reach those levels.

3. **Defined and pursued dreams/goals give direction to your life.**

   Without these life-directors, you will get discouraged and lack the persistence to keep going despite the challenges you face everyday in your sales office and model homes.

GOALS: THE WAY YOU SHAPE YOUR OWN LIFE

Every success you achieve has been, is and will be the result of your goals and dreams. If you want to become a *"slight-edge"* professional in the new home sales industry, you will have to become a *"slight-edge"* goal-setter and dreamer.

The important thing in life is not where you were or where you are but where you want to get!

Take a look at nine ways through which you can make goals work for you:

1. **Your goal is your target.**

   A goal is something specific you believe worth doing, and something you feel you can do. It's something you can get excited about.

   Life-goals enable you to CANCEL-CANCEL and screen out negatives. Goals help you to concentrate all your energies and resources in a single direction.

2. **Your goals must be specific.**

   The more specific a goal, the better your chances of reaching it. Do you want to be the top salesperson in your company? In your area? In your state? How detailed are you willing to become with your goals?

   People who set specific goals make things happen (PRO-ACTIVE); people who don't set goals end up waiting for something to happen (RE-ACTIVE).

3. **Your goals must be achievable.**
   A goal is not some vague "pie-in-the-sky" pipe dream or absurd fantasy. A good goal is one which causes you to stretch all your abilities, but one you're reasonably confident you can reach. Only you know the difference between a dream and a fantasy.

4. **Your goals must be practical.**
   To have meaning, goals must be broken down into three categories:

   - *Long-range goals* cover several years, but usually not more than 10.
   - *Intermediate goals* are set by breaking long-range goals down into annual, or semi-annual steps, always leading toward the long-range goals you have set.
   - *Short-range goals* come from breaking down your intermediate goals into monthly or weekly steps toward your long-range goals.

Everything you do has a definite impact on where you are going to be five or 10 years from now. Keep asking yourself where you want to be, then break that goal down into practical increments.

5. **Your goal needs a timetable.**
   If you want to start getting somewhere, set specific goals, give yourself definite deadlines for reaching them, then hold yourself to those deadlines.

6. **Goals must be important to you.**
   The key to all discipline is desire; the more you desire something, the easier self-discipline becomes. For example, it might be hard for you to boost your new home sales by 20% during the next year — just to prove to yourself you can do it. But if you plan this 20% boost as a means of achieving a dream (perhaps buying a new sports car or taking an exotic vacation) you may be surprised to find out what you can do.
   However, too many people buy the sports car on credit, then they are forced to boost their income by 20% just to make the payments. That is not self-discipline or goal-setting; it is bondage.

7. **Your goal is a promise to yourself.**
   Most of us are a lot better at keeping the promises we make to others than we are at keeping the promises we make to ourselves. Maybe that's why other people always seem to have more confidence in us than we have in ourselves.

Goals only work when you consider them to be promises you have made to yourself. Keep your commitments with the same tenacity as you would make good on an obligation to the bank or a close friend.

8. **Goals should cover every aspect of your life.**
   Many new home salespeople fail to reap the full benefit of setting goals because they confine them to their selling careers. For example, some of the best salespeople I have met are outstanding business and civic leaders, but are complete failures with their families.
   Likewise, some brilliant salespeople have marvelous minds, yet they completely ignore their needs for physical fitness.
   A good set of goals covers every area of life: career growth, family life, social development, mental/physical/spiritual well-being, financial security — every aspect which you feel is important.

9. **A goal should be a stepping stone.**
   Goals should enable you to keep expanding your horizons. One goal does not a career make. Success is the continuous journey along the upward path toward your goals.

What happens if you don't make your goals? If you gave it your best shot, you will have the deep inner satisfaction of knowing you tried. If you really wanted to reach a specific goal, you will probably set an even more difficult goal, double your efforts and keep going. People who set goals regularly find themselves doing that!

Even more, you will be miles ahead of where you would have been otherwise. Christopher Columbus determined to open a new trade route to India, but he missed it by thousands of miles. Instead, he discovered the "New World." Numerous cities, a country and even a national holiday commemorate Columbus — not bad for a "failure"!

WORKING HARD VERSUS WORKING SMART

There is a myth in American culture: "Those who work hardest are the ones who get rich." Often the opposite is more true. People who work *hard* tend to see the challenges looming in front of them. People who work *smart* concentrate on goals and objectives. For smart workers, tasks are mere steps to reach the most important levels.

The same principle applies to work habits. Hard working new home salespeople may talk about how many "things" they do each day, but smart working professionals focus on presentation-to-close ratios and how much they are achieving.

If you want to see a marked increase in your sales career, learn to plan your work carefully so every task you do will lead you closer to your goals.

The better you become at what you do, the more valuable you will become to your company and yourself.

PERSISTENCE

The obvious flaw in the way many people plan is this: They simply don't *"Follow-Through"* on their carefully-laid plans. As important as a well designed plan is, it is only a statement of what could be.

People who make plans work not only stick to those plans tenaciously, but they do it in an organized way.

Here are four ways to stick to your *"slight-edge"* professional plans:

1. **Get organized.**

   Most people waste vast amounts of time doing things in a disorganized way. The time you spend wading through clutter, looking for things you've misplaced, correcting mistakes, and following out-dated systems or procedures is time you could invest toward reaching your goals.

   I will discuss time-management, part of this extensive subject, in Chapter Sixteen.

2. **Monitor your progress.**

   Always think results, and constantly test to see that you are getting the results you want.

   One of the most effective tools for monitoring your progress is to keep a "to-do" list. I have mentioned this life-changer previously in the handbook.

   Consult your plan at the end of each day, and choose the most important things. Write down all of the things which you can reasonably expect to do. Next, rate each thing-to-do according to its priority level. The most important task becomes the number-one priority on your to-do list for the next day. The second most important, your number two priority, and so on.

   When you start out the next day, start with your number-one priority and concentrate on it until you either get it done or decide it can better be done later. When you have finished with number one, move on to number two.

   This is a convenient way of making sure you stay busy doing the right things, and it gives you a simple tool for measuring your progress every day.

3. **Check your schedule regularly.**

   Always include in your plans some regularly scheduled checkpoints at which you review your overall progress toward reaching your goals. It is important to realize that each missed deadline not only pushes each of your goals back that much more, but it can sabotage your entire plan.

4. **Keep your head and heart in the game.**
   This technique involves three basic elements:

   - Learn to distinguish between the important and urgent. Giving in to the urgent is called the "Fireperson Approach" — you are always running around putting out fires.
   - Find ways to do things better and in less time. The time you invest in looking for a better way to accomplish your tasks can be some of the most valuable time you invest.
   - Avoid the temptation to waste precious time when you discover you're ahead of schedule. An incredible amount of potential is lost by people who keep re-discovering "The Tortoise and Hare Syndrome."

Success in new home sales is possible for you! You can become a *"slight-edge"* professional if you determine to be better at planning your work, and working your plan.

A FINAL NOTE

Wishful thinking often keeps us from reaching goals. Too many people spend their lives trying to imagine what it would be like to live successfully. Wishful thinking sets you up for a negative mindset — "Why can't I ever get those things."

Replace wishful thinking by dreaming and setting written goals for yourself. Anyone can achieve success if they can learn to set long-range goals and break them into attainable, practical short and medium-range increments.

Whatever you want to have or become, you will only begin to fulfill your dreams by developing a concrete plan to make your dreams come true.

Set aside a definite time, during the next few days, to formulate a complete set of goals for every area of your life. Start with long-range goals, then break them down into intermediate and short-range goals.

STEPS

TO NEW HOME

SALES SUCCESS

1. *"Slight-edge"* professionals are generally better at being practical dreamers.

2. Short, mid and long-range goals shape your future, in new home sales and in all other areas of your life.

3. Your dreams and goals must be practical.

Chapter Sixteen

TIME — YOUR MOST VALUABLE ASSET

"Dost thou love life? Then do not squander time, for that's the stuff life is made of."

—BENJAMIN FRANKLIN [1]

TIME-MANAGEMENT

The major television networks diligently guard the prime-time hours from eight to eleven each night. They know this is when they have the largest audiences and, thus when they can make the most money from selling commercials.

Likewise, depending on your location and marketing strategies, you have certain times of each day and week which offer greater opportunities than any other time. Prime time for the salesperson is the precious intervals each day you spend actually selling.

Time-wasters rob you of your effectiveness during those peak hours.

WHAT'S THE NEED FOR TIME-MANAGEMENT?

Technically, you can't manage time because you have no control over it. And since you can't manufacture more hours in the day, all you can do is learn how to manage the use of time.

Therefore, when people speak of time management, they are actually talking about self-management.

To be successful in new home sales, you have to focus on your *goals,* not on *activities.*

If you constantly feel rushed and are still short of time, chances are pretty good that you need to do something about your personal time-management habits and practices.

EVALUATE YOUR TIME HABITS

The first step in managing your life is knowing precisely where the time goes. Most people have a general idea — so many hours are spent working, sleeping, eating and enjoying recreation. But *exactly* where do the hours go?

Time management experts suggest a very effective tactic for analyzing your time habits: over a specific period of time, keep a *detailed time log* for each 15 or 30-minute period of your working day and carefully analyze what you do with your time.

---

1. Poor Richard's Almanac, June 1746.

DISCOVER YOUR TIME-WASTING HABITS

Once you investigate trends in your schedule, you will also see that time-wasting habits can rob you of your most vital possession — time — and give little or nothing in return in terms of new home sales.

In a time-management study released by *USA Today*, research showed that during his or her career, the average American worker spends:

- Six months sitting at red lights.
- One year searching for belongings amid the clutter of home or office.
- Eight months opening junk mail.
- Two years playing "telephone tag".
- Three years attending meetings.
- Five years waiting in lines.
- Six years eating.

As you analyze your time-log for "thieves," watch specifically for these notorious "dirty dozen":

1. Procrastination.
2. Unnecessary routine tasks done because of habit.
3. Distractions or interruptions.
4. Inefficient use of the telephone.
5. Needless or lengthy meetings.
6. Excessive socializing.
7. Unclear organizational goals.
8. Inability to say "No!"
9. Trying to do too much or over-promising.
10. Red tape and paper shuffling.
11. Poor delegation.
12. Waiting for work to be finished by co-workers.

You may be able to add several time thieves from your lifestyle to the "dirty dozen." Brainstorm with your co-workers as you identify and begin to eliminate the time-wasters most prevalent in your sales office and in your life.

APPLY TIME-MANAGEMENT TECHNIQUES TO YOUR NEW HOME SALES CAREER

Here are 19 planning tips that I have taught to thousands of *"slight-edge"* professionals to get more done in less time:

1. Clarify your objectives.
2. Avoid activity traps.
3. Look for ways to work smarter, not harder.
4. Make sure that the first hour of your work day is a productive hour.

5. Eliminate at least one time-waster from your life each week.
6. Develop a strategy for handling interruptions.
7. Schedule quiet time for yourself to get things done.
8. Analyze your schedule. Ask yourself what would happen if you didn't get certain things done; if "nothing" is the answer, stop doing them.
9. Make a daily, weekly and monthly TO-DO list.
10. Allow flexibility in your day for the unexpected.
11. Be gracious with people, but firm with time. Learn how to say "No!"
12. Do it right the first time.
13. If crises keep reoccurring, learn to pre-act instead of reacting.
14. Eliminate, shorten, modify, combine or otherwise improve paperwork — try to handle paperwork only once.
15. Keep the clutter under control.
16. Take time to be a good listener — it saves time and prevents problems.
17. Show people your respect for their time, and they will usually return the favor.
18. Conquer procrastination.
19. Take time for yourself — time to dream, relax and "smell the roses."

Primarily, let me encourage you to balance time in all aspects of your life: spiritual, family, career, social, health, self-development and personal. Balance is the foundational structure for your *"slight-edge"* career as a new home salesperson.

GAIN CONTROL OF YOUR TIME

Remember, you can rationalize all time-wasters, but you cannot hide the fact that those moment-depleters make unmistakable statements about your goals, philosophy, values, intentions and needs.

Time-wasters have a high price-tag!

TIME VALUE CHART

ANNUAL INCOME	EACH HOUR IS WORTH	EACH MINUTE IS WORTH	AN HOUR A DAY FOR A YEAR IS WORTH
$20,000	$10.25	.17	$2,001
$25,000	$12.81	.21	$2,501
$30,000	$15.37	.26	$3,000
$35,000	$17.93	.30	$3,500
$40,000	$20.49	.34	$4,000
$50,000	$25.62	.43	$5,001
$75,000	$38.42	.64	$7,500
$100,000	$51.23	.85	$10,000
$125,000	$64.04	1.07	$12,501

Note: The table is based on 244 working days of eight hours each. By saving one hour each working day during a normal career, you can add the equivalent of six years of productivity.

A FINAL NOTE

There has never been a system devised that will work, unless you make it work.

Begin by keeping a time log. Analyze your time habits for the next two weeks. Then develop strategies to get better control of your time usage. Starting now, you can maximize your greatest assets in the weeks and years to come.

1. To become a better new home salesperson, seek to be a master at time-management.

2. Use a time-log to evaluate your scheduling habits.

3. Apply proven time-management techniques in your sales office, model home and every area of life.

4. Perfect the best habits through daily practice.

Chapter Seventeen

HOW TO STAY UP NO MATTER WHAT'S GOING DOWN

"To me, a winner is someone who recognizes his God-given talents, works his tail off to develop them into skills, and uses those skills to accomplish his goals. Even when I lost, I learned what my weaknesses were, and I went out the next day to turn those weaknesses into strengths."

—LARRY BIRD
Boston Celtics All-Star, and National Basketball Association MVP

LIVING LIFE TO THE FULLEST

I love the title of Neil Eskelin's book, *Yes-Yes Living in a No-No World.* That phrase perfectly describes what your life must encompass as a new home salesperson.

You see, there are plenty of negative forces which come against you — turndowns and conflicts. You don't always have control over the negatives. But you can determine your attitude.

One of the most startling discoveries of life happens when you realize that you have the power to choose what kind of day you are going to have. Each day comes to you neutral: it is neither up or down. You choose whether you will be positive or negative. The mood of your day is not set by circumstances, by other people, by tasks you have to do, by events that happen along the way. It is set by one thing — your *attitude!*

You may not always be able to control what happens to you, but you can always control the way you react to what happens.

BECOME AN "INNER WINNER"

Only you can motivate yourself. In the final analysis, all motivation is self-motivation. Let me suggest five insights into motivating yourself, not just in the model homes, but throughout every area of your life:

1. **An UP day starts the night before.**

   Spend time each night reflecting on the good things that have happened that day. Lay out your clothes. Check "to do" lists for the next day.

   John D. Rockefeller once told how he ended each day. He said that he always emptied his pockets very slowly, the last thing before he retired. As he took things out of his pockets, he made a conscious effort to empty his mind of all worry, anxiety and negative thoughts.

2. **Get up and at 'em.**

The most important hour in each day is not the "happy hour" — it is the first hour you are awake. That first hour sets the pace for the remainder of the day.

Starting out the day on a positive note sets a tone for positive thoughts all day — the emotional version of the law of inertia.

3. **Keep your goals in sight.**

When Florence Chadwick set out from the coast of France to make her historic swim in 1952, she was full of hope and courage. The lone swimmer was surrounded by boats filled with newsmen, well-wishers, and some skeptics. For years she had trained vigorously, but as she neared the coast of England, a heavy fog settled in and the waters became increasingly cold and choppy.

"Come on Florence, you can make it!" urged her mother as she handed some food to her. "It's only a few more miles! You're ahead of schedule!" But Florence was exhausted and finally asked to be pulled aboard a boat. She was heart-broken; especially when she discovered how close she'd come to her goal.

"I'm not making excuses," she later told reporters, "But I think I could have made it if I could have only seen my goal."

But Florence determined to try again. This time, however, she added a new dimension to her daily training. She studied the shoreline of England where she expected to land, and memorized every feature of that famous seacoast. Each day as she swam, she would replay that mental image of her goal.

On her second attempt, she again ran into the ravages of nature, but something was different. She swam with greater vigor and determination. She became the first woman in history to swim the English channel, and set a record that will probably stand forever!

What was that difference? She later said that it was because she was able to keep her goal clearly in focus in her mind, even when she could not see it with her eyes.

Your goals are only as good as the way they are focused in your mind. Visualize yourself reaching your goals and replay that mental picture. Then, no matter what arises, you will be able to keep your sense of direction.

4. **Keep building yourself up.**

One millionaire has been asked many times why he succeeded when people he grew up with never made it. His simple answer is: "I guess I just had more reasons to get rich than they did."

One of the best ways to keep yourself motivated is to focus as many reasons as you can think of to succeed, and to keep reminding yourself of all those reasons.

As motivational speaker Jim Rohn often says, "A person can accomplish the most incredible things, if he has enough reasons to."

5. **Play the game to win.**
   Keep reminding yourself that you don't have to run second to anybody. To life's champions, it's never enough to simply be glad to be in the game — they're always in it to win it!

KEEP YOURSELF UP

No one is the best at everything all the time. By definition, you cannot succeed unless you encounter challenges. Sometimes you will fail, perhaps miserably. But the greatest, reoccurring question is not, "Will I keep getting knocked down" but "Will I keep getting up?"

The record books are filled with stories about people who failed time and again, but ultimately succeeded:

- Babe Ruth held the record for strike-outs long before he set the homerun record.
- Henry Ford forgot a reverse gear in his first car.
- Thomas Edison tried thousands of materials before he found the one which made his incandescent light work.

Many of these successful people had mediocre talents, most struggled against overwhelming odds, and all had many reasons to give up. But they kept going, despite the losses, until they overcame the odds. Will you? Can you simply refuse to stay down? Can you focus on results, not on problems? Will you be able to keep yourself motivated?

History is full of stories of people who did what everyone thought was impossible. They did it because they connected with an inner power that comes only from a burning desire.

Cy Young, for whom professional baseball's most coveted award for pitcher of the year is named, was a great star, yet he only won 511 big league games out of the 906 that he pitched — just a few more than half.

To be an outstanding success in any endeavor, it is not necessary to be right all the time. If you are right more than half the time, you may win a gold medal, make a million dollars, invent a new computer chip or develop a cure for a dreaded disease or join the top 5% of all new home salespeople.

The idea is to keep doing the things that successful people do!

ENTHUSIASM FUELS SELF-MOTIVATION

Enthusiasm is a strong word with a rich heritage. It comes from an ancient Greek word "entheos" which is loosely translated "inspired by the gods." Originally, the word was coined to express admiration for Olympic athletes who performed what seemed to be superhuman feats. It literally means a person who performs as if he or she "has a god inside them." Modern dictionaries define it as "warmth of feeling, keen interest, fervor."

Your enthusiasm comes from a combination of two deep, inner convictions:

1. **Being captivated by an ideal.**

   True enthusiasm springs from a strong belief that *something* is worth doing to the best of your ability.

   "Nothing great was ever accomplished without enthusiasm," said Ralph Waldo Emerson.

   If you want to see your life really take off, give yourself completely to that deepest urge within you; lose yourself in a cause you consider worthy of your very best.

   Far too many people today are looking for some group, or some society, to give them something worth living and dying for. Great societies come from great people with great ideals; not vice versa.

2. **Having a deep conviction that you can accomplish something.**

   Only you can decide whether or not to listen to your "inner winner" dreams. Only you can make that final decision to reach for your goals.

   Will you?

   Remember: All *change* is not *growth*, just like all *motion* is not *forward*.

A FINAL NOTE

Self-motivation and enthusiasm comes from the deep, inner conviction that you can succeed as a new home salesperson — no matter what the odds may be.

With *THE OFFICIAL HANDBOOK FOR NEW HOME SALESPEOPLE*, you have in your hands the key strategies needed to become a *"slight-edge"* success in our industry.

How do you stay UP in a DOWN world? Only you, and you alone, can control who you are from the inside out.

Based on working with thousands of salespeople, I have no doubt that you can achieve phenomenal success. But only YOU can decide whether or not you will do whatever it takes to become a highly-paid, *"slight-edge"*, new home sales professional.

Do it!

1. You can stay UP in a DOWN world by living life to the fullest and being an "inner winner."

2. Keep yourself up by realizing that failure is always a part of succeeding.

3. Build self-motivation through enthusiasm.

Recommended Reading List

FOR NEW HOME SALESPEOPLE

"Resolve to edge in a little reading every day. If you gain but 15 minutes a day, it will make itself felt at the end of a year."

—HORACE MANN
"Father of American Education"

ALBRECHT, KARL, and RON ZEMKE, *Service America!* Homewood, IL: Dow Jones-Irwin.

BETTGER, FRANK, *How I Raised Myself from Failure to Success in Selling.* New York: Simon & Schuster.

BROADWELL, MARTIN M., *Moving Up to Supervision.* New York: Wiley-Interscience Publications.

FAST, JULIUS, *Body Language.*

GARD, GRANT G., *Championship Selling.*

GIRARD, JOE, *How to Sell Anything to Anybody.*

HOPKINS, TOM, *How to Master the Art of Selling.*

HOPKINS, TOM, *The Official Guide to Success.*

KENNEDY, DANIELLE. *Super Natural Selling for Everyday People.*

KOUZES, JAMES M., and BARRY Z. POSNER, *The Leadership Challenge.* San Francisco: Jossey-Bass Publishers.

LEVINSON, HARRY, *Executive.* Cambridge, MA: Harvard University Press.

MACKAY, HARVEY, *Swim with the Sharks Without Being Eaten Alive.* New York: William Morrow and Company.

MALLOY, JOHN T., *Dress for Success.*

MCCORMACK, MARK H., *What They Don't Teach You at Harvard Business School.* New York: Bantam.

PEALE, NORMAN, *The Power of Positive Thinking.*

QUBEIN, NIDO, *Get the Best from Yourself.* Englewood Cliffs, NJ: Prentice-Hall.

QUBEIN, NIDO, *Professional Selling Techniques.* New York: Berkley.

RAY, MICHAEL, and ROCHELLE MYERS. *Creativity in Business.* New York: Doubleday.

SCHWARTZ, DAVID J., PH.D., *The Magic of Thinking Big.* Englewood Cliffs, NJ: Prentice-Hall.

STONE, DAVE, *New Home Sales.* Chicago: Real Estate Education Company.

TARKENTON, FRAN, with TAD TULEJA, *How to Motivate People.* New York: Harper & Row.

VON OECH, ROGER, PH.D., *A Whack on the Side of the Head.* New York: Warner Books.

COHEN, HERB, *You Can Negotiate Anything.*

WAITLEY, DENIS, PH.D., *The Winner's Edge.* Old Tappan, NJ: Fleming Revell Co.

WALTERS, DOTTIE, *The Selling Power of a Woman.*

WHEELER, ELMER, *How to Sell Yourself to Others.*

ZIGLAR, ZIG, *Zig Ziglar's Secrets of Closing a Sale.*

ZIGLAR, ZIG, *See You At the Top.*

New Home Salespeople

ONE FINAL NOTE

"Far better is it to dare mighty things,
to win glorious triumphs, even though
checkered by failure, than to rank with
those poor spirits who neither enjoy much
nor suffer much, because they live in the gray
twilight that knows not victory nor defeat."

—THEODORE ROOSEVELT

THE FINAL THOUGHT

"If you keep on thinking the way you've
always been thinking, you'll keep on getting
what you've always been getting!"
Is that enough?

—BOB SCHULTZ

About the Author

BOB SCHULTZ, is Founder and President of New Home Specialist Inc., a company which creates, and publishes solutions oriented programs and management systems, serving home builders, developers, housing manufacturers and Realtors throughout North America.

With more than three decades of practical, hands-on experience in all phases of new home sales and management, he is widely recognized as North America's foremost new home sales and management expert. Beginning in new home sales as the top on-line salesperson in his early twenties for one of the largest volume builders in Florida, to President of companies responsible for the sales of more than three thousand homes in more than 30 communities, with a present day dollar volume in excess of *two billion*, he is uniquely qualified.

Bob is a member of and has served as a trustee and Vice-Chairman of the Sales and Marketing Council of the National Association of Home Builders and as a Trustee and Vice-President of its Institute of Residential Marketing. He is a faculty member of the NAHB's Home Builders Institute and has served as Chairman of the NAHB's National Sales and Marketing Council's Builder-Realtor Relations Committee.

He has been recognized for his expertise by being named "Sales Director of the Year" by both The Florida Home Builders Association and The Builders Association of South Florida, and has received special recognition by the National Association of Home Builders as "Marketing Director of the Year, Large Volume".

A member of the National Speakers Association, he is the only consultant exclusively serving the home building industry to receive its coveted CSP (Certified Speaking Professional) designation.

He is the author of, ***The Official Handbook for New Home Salespeople***, ***Smart Selling℠ Techniques***, "The Five Minute Professional" audiocassette series and The Official New Home Sales Development System®, a video learning program.

As the industry innovator in education, New Home Specialist has created the Bob Schultz Inner Circle, an elite group of sales and marketing management professionals from companies across North America. He leads them in a series of retreats, workshops and teleconference meetings to raise their level of skills in a synergistic setting. A pioneer in nationally produced educational seminars, he created and presented in partnership with Builder Magazine for its BUILDER University, a series of six sales and sales management seminars, known as *Serious Sales Training℠* and *Serious Sales Management℠* and *Smart Selling℠* and *Smart Sales Management℠*. Featured along with Bob at these seminars have been other renowned speakers such as Zig Ziglar, Brian Tracy, The Covey Leadership and Nido Qubein. More than 1,000 new home sales professionals from around the world have graduated from these courses, as well as from his newest industry-wide programs.

For more information about how New Home Specialist Education Systems and Bob Schultz' seminars and consulting expertise can help you achieve the results you demand, contact:

New Home Specialist Education Systems
2300 Glades Road, Suite 400 West
Boca Raton, Florida 33431 USA
561/368-1151
561/368-1171 (Fax)
E-mail: info@newhomespecialist.com
Visit our website at: www.newhomespecialist.com

RESOURCE GUIDE

HE NEW HOME SALES PROFESSIONAL LIBRARY

is library is essential for professionals at all levels.

The Five Minute Professional CD Series
By Bob Schultz, MIRM, CSP, with Roland Nairnsey, CSP

The Official Handbook for New Home Salespeople
By Bob Schultz, MIRM, CSP

Smart Selling Techniques
By Bob Schultz, MIRM, CSP

Selling to Multicultural Home Buyers.
By Michael Lee, CRS, GRI, CSP

THE NEW HOME SALES MANAGEMENT SYSTEMS

Each system manual includes a CD-ROM containing customizable templates for letters, scripts and interviews.

- THE OFFICIAL NEW HOME SALES RECRUITING SYSTEM℠
  By Bob Schultz, MIRM, CSP
- THE OFFICIAL SYSTEM FOR NEW HOME SALES FOLLOW-THROUGH®
  By Steve Hoffacker, MIRM, CSP
- THE OFFICIAL SYSTEM FOR NEW HOME SALES CONSUMER RESEARCH
  By Steve Hoffacker, MIRM, CSP
- FRANCHISE REPORTS SOFTWARE
- MANAGING FOR SUCCESS (MFS) PERSONALITY STYLE REPORTS (Call for pricing)

TO ORDER
VISIT OUR ON-LINE STORE AT
www.newhomespecialist.com
Quantity discounts apply

New Home Specialist Inc.
2300 Glades Road • Suite 400W • Boca Raton, FL 33431 • Phone: (561) 368-1151 • Fax: (561) 368-1171
Email: info@newhomespecialist.com • Website: www.newhomespecialist.com

Notes

Special Free Offer

For readers of The Official Handbook for New Home Salespeople

New Home Specialist℠ is dedicated to the new home sales profession. We are educators, trainers and consultants to hundreds of companies throughout North America and to thousands of new home sales professionals around the world.

Bob Schultz, MIRM, CSP, is the founder and president of New Home Specialist Inc. With Bob's extensive experience and under his leadership, the company creates education and training systems that are unequaled in the industry. Our company publishes world-class resources such as books, management systems, video and audiocassette learning programs, which we are proud to offer, as a part of ***The Official New Home Sales Development System.***® Each is packed with powerful, effective and proven concepts, strategies, techniques and methods, that when applied, will accelerate you and your team along the road of personal and professional achievement.

If **YOU** would like access to the most recent live recorded presentations and articles containing current and insightful information by Bob Schultz, or one of our other New Home Specialist associate consultants and facilitators, and to receive our bi-weekly ***Strategies Newsletter*** via e-mail, all on a complimentary basis, simply let us know who **YOU** are!

Print Name:______________________________

Title:______________________________

Company:______________________________

Address:______________________________

City:______________ State:__________ Zip Code:__________

Phone:______________ Fax:______________

Email:______________ Website:______________

Where and when did you acquire The Official Handbook for New

Home Salespeople?______________________________

Please send to:
New Home Specialist Inc.
2300 Glades Road ✦ Suite 400 W
Boca Raton, Florida 33431

-or-

Call or fax:
Phone: (561) 368-1151
Fax: (561) 368-1171
Email: info@newhomespecialist.com
Website: www.newhomespecialist.com

Notes